ANYTHING BUT VANILLA

ANYTHING BUT VANILLA

The Roadmap to Differentiation

in a World Full of Bland Brands

MARCOS G. FIGUEIRA

Anything but Vanilla: The Roadmap to Differentiation in a World Full of Bland Brands

Copyright © 2024 by Marcos G. Figueira

All rights reserved. No part of this publication may be used in any manner whatsoever without written permission except in the case of brief quotations embodied in critical articles or reviews.

This publication is designed to provide accurate and authoritative in regard to the subject matter covered. While the publisher and author have used their best efforts in preparing this book, they make no representations warranties with respect to the accuracy or completeness of the contents of this book and specifically disclaim any implied warranties of merchantability or fitness for a particular purpose. Neither the publisher nor the author shall be liable for any loss of profit or any other comercial damages, including but not limited to special, incidental, consequential, personal, or other damages.

For information contact: email@marcosfigueira.com
https://marcosfigueira.com

Figueira, Marcos G.

Anything but Vanilla: The Roadmap to Differentiation in a World Full of Bland Brands

Edition: 1st ed.

Publication: USA: Independently published.

ISBN: 9798344439051

1. Business. 2. Marketing. 3. Management. 4. Branding. 5. Strategy. 6. Entrepreneurship. 7. Startups.

TABLE OF CONTENTS

TABLE OF CONTENTS — 5
INTRODUCTION — 7
Why Differentiate or Die

CHAPTER 01 — 17
The Foundation of Differentiation

CHAPTER 02 — 33
The Myths of Uniqueness

CHAPTER 03 — 47
Crafting a Unique Value Proposition

CHAPTER 04 — 63
The Emotional Edge

CHAPTER 05 — 81
Creating Brand Assets That Stick

CHAPTER 06 — 99
Positioning Your Brand

CHAPTER 07 — 115
Consistency is Queen

CHAPTER 08 127
Digital-First Branding

CHAPTER 09 141
Standing Out in Sameness

CHAPTER 10 153
Sustaining Differentiation

CONCLUSION 161
Differentiation is Forever

REFERENCES 169
ABOUT THE AUTHOR 173
THANK YOU! 174

INTRODUCTION

WHY DIFFERENTIATE OR DIE

Stand out or get lost

It is undeniable—we are surrounded by bland, vanilla brands. Walk down any aisle, scroll through any social media feed, and you'll see the same thing over and over again: brands blending into the background, indistinguishable from one another. But here's the harsh truth: if you're not standing out, you're already losing. The marketplace doesn't have time for "average" anymore. It only rewards brands that are bold enough to be unforgettable.

In a world where everyone is shouting for attention, playing it safe is the quickest way to vanish. You might think that casting a wide net will catch more fish, but the opposite is true. The broader your appeal, the less impact you make. People don't remember brands that try to please everyone—they remember the ones that speak directly to them, the ones that *dare* to be different.

The illusion of safety

It's easy to see why brands fall into the trap of playing it safe. It feels comfortable. Familiar. But safety is an illusion—especially in today's hyper-competitive market. The brands that are afraid to push boundaries, afraid to offend, afraid to take a stand, are the ones that fade into obscurity.

Look at the cereal aisle as an example. Amidst a hundred brands offering slight variations of the same thing, the ones that thrive are the ones that make you stop and pay attention. Think of the bold packaging of a brand like Lucky Charms compared to the muted tones of generic corn flakes. People don't want to choose something boring; they want something exciting. Something that grabs their attention and makes them feel something.

The science of attention

Our brains are wired to notice what's different. It's a survival instinct—our minds are constantly scanning for what stands out, what breaks the pattern. It's no wonder then that brands that dare to disrupt the norm are the ones that stick in our minds. When Apple launched its iconic "Think Different" campaign, it didn't just sell computers—it challenged the entire notion of what technology could be.

The psychology here is simple: we remember what makes us feel something. We remember brands that inspire us, challenge us, or even provoke us. The brands that stay in our minds are the ones that don't just meet expectations—they shatter them.

Forget being liked. Aim to be remembered.

There's a dangerous misconception that brands need to be liked by everyone to succeed. But the reality is, trying to appeal to the masses almost always results in being ignored by all. The goal isn't to be liked by everyone. It's to be remembered by the right people. To be remarkable means being polarizing at times, and that's okay.

Being unforgettable is far more valuable than being universally liked.

Think of Harley-Davidson. Not everyone dreams of riding a loud, rebellious motorcycle. But for the people who do, Harley isn't just a brand—it's a symbol of freedom and rebellion. That's what it means to carve out a brand identity that people can't ignore. You don't need everyone's approval—just the right audience's undying loyalty.

Distraction is your enemy

In the digital age, attention is more fragmented than ever. Brands are fighting for split-second moments of recognition. In this battle, it's not the safe, middle-of-the-road brands that win. It's the bold, daring brands that force people to stop scrolling and take notice.

Dollar Shave Club didn't break into the market by having the best razors. They broke in by creating one of the most memorable ad campaigns ever—a brash, hilarious video that went viral and turned an entire industry on its head. They weren't the first razor subscription service, but they were the first to make a lasting impression. And that made all the difference.

Pick a lane

The most successful brands know exactly who they are, who they serve, and where they're going. They don't try to be everything to everyone. They choose a lane, stick to it, and go full speed ahead. When Nike tells you to "Just Do It," they aren't just selling shoes. They're selling an attitude, a mindset of relentless ambition. It's a message that might not resonate with everyone, but for those it does, it hits hard.

Being decisive about your brand's identity is crucial. Waffling between different messages, tones, and target audiences will only confuse consumers and dilute your impact. To stand out, you need clarity—both in your message and in your purpose.

What comes next?

Being bold isn't about taking wild risks for the sake of it. It's about understanding that in a marketplace filled with noise, standing out is the only way forward. Brands that refuse to differentiate will be left behind, fading into the background of irrelevance. But the ones that dare to disrupt, to push the boundaries, to be remarkable—they are the ones that people will remember long after the rest have disappeared.

So, what kind of brand do you want to be? The one people forget? Or the one they can't stop talking about?

The choice is yours, but make it fast. Because the next chapter is going to reveal the fate of those brands that didn't make the right choice in time.

Lessons from history: Why brands fail to differentiate

History is littered with brands that were once household names, now relegated to distant memories. These brands didn't fail because they lacked quality or resources; they failed because they couldn't—or wouldn't—differentiate. The marketplace is unforgiving to those who blend in, and history shows us that staying the same is far riskier than evolving.

Consider Blockbuster, a giant that seemed unstoppable at its peak. With thousands of stores worldwide, Blockbuster dominated the video rental industry. But when Netflix introduced a new model—streaming—Blockbuster hesitated. Instead of embracing change, they clung to their outdated model. The result? A slow, painful decline. Blockbuster had the chance to differentiate by adapting to changing consumer habits, but they failed to seize it. Netflix didn't have a larger budget or more resources; it had a willingness to be different, to challenge the norm.

Playing it safe: The silent killer

Many brands that fade into obscurity do so not because they lacked innovation but because they were afraid to use it. Kodak is another tragic example. A company that invented the digital camera, yet feared it would cannibalize its film business. Rather than embracing the digital future, Kodak tried to protect its legacy, and in doing so, sealed its fate. The irony is that Kodak had the innovation it needed to survive but lacked the boldness to lead with it.

Playing it safe might feel like the responsible choice, but in a world that rewards differentiation, safety is often the silent killer. History has repeatedly shown that the refusal to evolve in the face of new competition or technology is a surefire way to fade into irrelevance.

The myth of brand loyalty

Another reason brands fail to differentiate is a blind belief in customer loyalty. Many once-successful brands assumed that because they had a loyal customer base, they didn't need to change. Sears, a retail giant for decades, fell into this trap. The company believed its name and history would carry it through the retail transformation of the 21st century. But as consumer preferences shifted and competitors like Amazon and Walmart embraced e-commerce and innovation, Sears clung to its brick-and-mortar empire. What they failed to recognize was that loyalty is conditional. Consumers are loyal until something better comes along. And when brands fail to offer something different, something better *always* comes along.

Consumers aren't attached to the past; they're focused on what's most convenient, most relevant, and most exciting in the present. Brands that fail to differentiate are betting that their past success will guarantee future relevance. That bet rarely pays off.

Death by commoditization

Commoditization is the final nail in the coffin for brands that fail to differentiate. When brands don't stand out, they get reduced to nothing more than a commodity, fighting in a race to the bottom on price. Remember Blackberry? Once the leader in mobile communication, they found themselves unable to compete when smartphones became the new standard. Their brand, once synonymous with security and professionalism, became just another phone on the shelf.

The failure wasn't in their technology; it was in their refusal to evolve their brand identity. Apple and Samsung entered the market with a vision of the future, one where phones were not just for work but for life, for play, and for connection. Blackberry's inability to differentiate beyond its initial offering led to its downfall.

Reinvention or extinction

The lesson here is simple: brands that fail to differentiate inevitably face extinction. Those that survive are the ones that constantly reinvent themselves, embracing change rather than resisting it. Take LEGO, a brand that was on the verge of collapse in the early 2000s. Sales were plummeting, and the company seemed destined for failure. Instead of giving up, LEGO focused on what made them unique—creativity, imagination, and play. They expanded their brand into new arenas like movies, video games, and theme parks, all while staying true to their core. The result? A remarkable turnaround that made LEGO one of the most beloved brands in the world today.

Brands that survive the test of time understand that differentiation isn't a one-time effort—it's a continuous process of reinvention. Those that rest on their laurels, believing their current success will carry them into the future, are setting themselves up for failure.

We will soon explore how to escape the commodity trap—a critical move for any brand aiming to survive and thrive. But first, take a moment to consider: is your brand truly different, or is it coasting on past successes? Because in today's marketplace, standing still is the same as moving backwards.

The cost of being average

Mediocrity comes with a price tag. The problem is, most brands don't realize how costly "average" is until it's too late. Being average might seem safe. It's comfortable. But in the world of branding, comfortable is the enemy of growth. When you're just another option on the shelf, your customers have no reason to choose you over your competitors. In fact, they probably won't even notice you.

What many companies don't understand is that being average doesn't just prevent you from standing out—it actually pushes you into obscurity. It makes you forgettable. And forgettable brands don't thrive. They don't survive. They fade away, slowly drained of relevance and revenue by the ones that dared to be different.

The race to the bottom

When your brand is average, you're competing on price. It's the race to the bottom, and nobody wins. Instead of focusing on creating value, you're stuck in an endless cycle of discounting, price cuts, and desperate promotions. Sure, this might drive some short-term sales, but it's a losing strategy in the long run.

Consider the retail apocalypse that's claimed brands like J.C. Penney and RadioShack. These were companies that fell into the trap of being average, with no real point of difference from their competitors. What happened? As e-commerce giants like Amazon began to dominate with lower prices and better convenience, these once-strong brands crumbled, unable to offer anything compelling enough to keep customers loyal.

When you compete on price alone, there will always be someone willing to go lower. And that's a game that only ends one way—at the bottom.

Average brands, invisible brands

One of the most damaging aspects of being average is invisibility. If your brand doesn't stand out, it's like you don't exist. Sure, you might have a solid product or service, but so do a hundred other brands. In a crowded marketplace, being good isn't good enough.

Think about the last time you bought toothpaste. Did you spend time analyzing the options, or did you grab the one you've been using for years without a second thought? That's the danger of being an average brand—you become part of the background. Consumers don't seek you out. They don't talk about you. And when a more exciting option comes along, they'll drop you in a heartbeat because you haven't given them a reason to stay.

The cost of lost loyalty

When a brand is average, customer loyalty becomes incredibly fragile. Consumers aren't loyal to brands that are just "fine." They're loyal to brands that make them feel something—whether it's excitement, trust, or a sense of belonging. Average brands don't evoke those emotions. Instead, they sit in a middle ground that's safe, but uninspiring.

Look at what happened to once-mighty brands like Nokia. At one point, Nokia was the global leader in mobile phones. Their products were reliable, sturdy, and functional—basically, the definition of "good enough." But when Apple entered the scene with the iPhone, offering not just a phone but a new lifestyle, Nokia's market share plummeted. Their product was fine. Apple's product was *exciting*. And that difference in emotion made all the difference in loyalty.

Missed opportunities

Being average also means missing out on opportunities for growth and innovation. When your brand is stuck in the safe zone, you stop pushing boundaries, stop trying new things, and stop evolving. This mindset limits your ability to adapt to changes in the market, leaving you vulnerable to disruption from more daring competitors.

Blockbuster's refusal to innovate with streaming technology is a prime example. They had the resources, the market dominance, and the customer base to own the future of entertainment. But their average approach—sticking with their brick-and-mortar rental model—left them scrambling to catch up once Netflix proved that streaming was the future. Blockbuster could have led the change, but instead, they became irrelevant.

The hidden cost of stagnation

Average isn't just boring. It's dangerous. It lulls companies into a false sense of security, where they think they're doing enough to get by. But "getting by" is never a sustainable strategy. Sooner or later, a brand that refuses to push beyond mediocrity will stagnate. And stagnation is just another word for decline.

Meanwhile, bolder brands are constantly evolving, experimenting, and improving. They understand that staying relevant means staying dynamic. Consider Microsoft's reinvention. For years, the brand felt stagnant—overshadowed by younger, more innovative tech companies. But under Satya Nadella's leadership, Microsoft shifted focus, embraced cloud computing, and rekindled its pioneering spirit. The result? A resurgence that saw them become one of the most valuable companies in the world again.

The difference is stark: average brands decline. Remarkable brands adapt, evolve, and grow.

A choice to be made

The cost of being average is far greater than most brands realize. It's not just about lost sales or forgotten marketing campaigns—it's about long-term survival. Brands that don't push beyond mediocrity are doomed to fight for scraps in an increasingly competitive world.

The real question is: Are you willing to pay that price?

Because next, we're diving into the deeper psychology of differentiation—what it really means to stand out, and why brands that embrace it thrive, while those that don't... well, you've seen how that story ends.

CHAPTER 01

THE FOUNDATION OF DIFFERENTIATION

What differentiation really means

Differentiation is more than just being different for the sake of it. In a market crowded with noise and distraction, true differentiation is about creating an identity so unique, so unmistakably *you*, that consumers can't help but notice. It's not about wild stunts or gimmicks; it's about consistently offering something your competitors simply can't.

At its core, differentiation is about making a promise to your customers that no one else can make. It's the DNA of your brand—the thing that, if removed, would make you just another player in the field. Differentiation isn't just what sets you apart; it's why people will choose you over the thousands of other options out there. It's about having a reason to exist in the mind of your customer.

Beyond being "different"

Too often, brands believe that being different is enough. But difference without substance is just a gimmick. Sure, you can paint your product in neon colors or give it a quirky name, but unless those changes add real value, they'll fade into irrelevance. The marketplace is full of brands that tried to stand out with surface-level differentiation and failed because they didn't offer anything of substance beneath the packaging.

True differentiation requires a deeper dive. It's not about being different for the sake of it—it's about offering something your audience genuinely needs or wants, in a way that no one else can. Think of Tesla. It didn't differentiate itself by just making electric cars; it redefined what people thought a car could be. Tesla tapped into a vision of the future that went beyond transportation. Their differentiation lies not only in their product but in their mission to push boundaries and accelerate the world's transition to sustainable energy.

The emotional connection

One key element of successful differentiation is emotional resonance. The most iconic brands don't just sell products—they sell ideas, emotions, and lifestyles. Apple isn't just about sleek designs and powerful tech; it's about creativity, individuality, and breaking free from the status quo. When you buy an Apple product, you're not just buying a phone or a laptop—you're buying into a mindset, a philosophy of thinking differently.

Differentiation is powerful because it connects with people on an emotional level. And when emotions are involved, loyalty follows. It's no coincidence that brands that create a strong emotional bond with their customers—like Nike, Harley-Davidson, and Coca-Cola—end up with armies of die-hard fans who stick with them for life.

Functional vs. emotional differentiation

There are two major types of differentiation: functional and emotional. Functional differentiation is all about what your product or service *does* better than anyone else's. This could be faster delivery, better quality, lower price, or unique features that no one else offers. Functional differentiation is important, but it's not always enough to create long-lasting loyalty.

Emotional differentiation, on the other hand, is about how your brand *makes people feel*. It's the secret sauce that takes your brand from good to unforgettable. When you evoke emotions, you're not just giving your customers a reason to buy—you're giving them a reason to stay.

Take Harley-Davidson, for example. There's no shortage of motorcycle brands on the market, but Harley isn't just selling a machine on two wheels. They're selling freedom, rebellion, and the open road. It's that emotional connection that makes Harley riders fiercely loyal, proudly showing off their Harleys as symbols of their identity.

The trap of imitation

One of the biggest threats to differentiation is the temptation to imitate. Brands see what's working for their competitors and think, "If it works for them, it'll work for us." But copying someone else's strategy is the quickest way to get lost in the crowd. The brands that thrive are the ones that stay true to their own identity, even if it means taking risks or going against the grain.

Remember when Pepsi tried to copy Coca-Cola's branding during the "New Coke" era? It didn't go well. Pepsi's attempts to mimic Coke's success resulted in a product that felt forced, inauthentic, and ultimately alienated their audience. The lesson? Differentiation is about owning your space in the market, not borrowing someone else's.

Authenticity is non-negotiable

Consumers today have an uncanny ability to sniff out inauthenticity. They know when a brand is trying too hard or when its message doesn't align with its actions. Authenticity is key to meaningful differentiation. If your brand's actions don't match its message, you'll lose trust—and in today's market, trust is one of the most valuable currencies.

Take Patagonia as a case in point. The brand's differentiation lies in its commitment to environmental activism. This isn't just a marketing angle; it's deeply embedded in everything they do—from their supply chain to their product lines. Consumers trust Patagonia because the brand walks the talk, and that authenticity creates a level of loyalty that's hard to rival.

Differentiation is a commitment

Differentiation isn't a one-time strategy—it's a long-term commitment. Brands that successfully differentiate themselves don't just stand out once; they build a reputation for consistently delivering on their promise. It's not about jumping on the latest trend or making flashy moves. It's about staying true to what makes you unique, even as the market shifts and trends come and go.

The road to differentiation is challenging. It requires introspection, risk-taking, and a deep understanding of your audience. But for brands willing to make the commitment, the rewards are immense.

Think about it: would you rather be a brand that fades into the background, or one that stands the test of time because it dared to be different?

Next, we'll dive into the psychology of standing out—because understanding what makes people take notice is half the battle.

The psychology of standing out

Why do certain brands capture our attention while others fade into the background? It's not just about having a great product or a flashy logo. The secret to standing out lies deep in the human brain. There's a science behind why some brands are unforgettable, while others are ignored, and it all comes down to understanding how people process and react to the world around them.

Human beings are wired to notice what's different. Our brains are constantly scanning for novelty, for something that breaks the pattern. In prehistoric times, this ability was a survival mechanism—our ancestors needed to be alert to anything unusual that could pose a threat or offer an opportunity. Today, that same instinct drives us to notice the brands, products, and ideas that challenge the status quo. Simply put, if you want to stand out, you need to tap into this basic human instinct.

Novelty triggers attention

The brain is designed to ignore the familiar and focus on what's new or unexpected. This is why we stop and notice things that are out of the ordinary. Brands that break with convention trigger this response, making them impossible to ignore. Think about the first time you saw an Apple product with its sleek, minimalist design. In a world of clunky, button-filled gadgets, Apple's products felt like something from the future. That sense of novelty is what drew people in.

But novelty alone isn't enough. It's the first step, sure, but to sustain attention, you need more. Your brand can't just be different for the sake of it. There needs to be depth—something that keeps people engaged long after the initial shock of the new has worn off.

Creating emotional impact

Standing out isn't just about being visually different. It's about creating an emotional impact. Humans are emotional creatures, and we remember experiences that make us *feel* something. Whether it's joy, nostalgia, excitement, or even fear, brands that connect on an emotional level stick with us longer.

Take Coca-Cola's "Share a Coke" campaign. By replacing their iconic logo with people's names, they turned a simple bottle of soda into a personal, emotional experience. Suddenly, it wasn't just a drink—it was a connection, a moment of shared joy. That emotional resonance turned a generic product into something deeply personal, and it paid off in spades.

When brands understand the emotions that drive their audience, they can create experiences that go beyond the product itself. It's not enough to just be seen—you need to be *felt*.

The power of storytelling

One of the most effective ways to trigger emotional responses is through storytelling. Humans are hardwired for stories. From ancient myths to modern advertising, stories have always been a way to make sense of the world. They help us relate, connect, and remember. Brands that tell compelling stories tap into this primal need, making themselves memorable in a sea of forgettable products.

Think of Nike's "Just Do It" campaign. It's more than just a tagline—it's a story of perseverance, struggle, and victory. It's a story that athletes around the world can see themselves in. Nike doesn't just sell shoes; they sell the idea that you, too, can achieve greatness. And that story is what makes the brand so powerful.

A great story doesn't need to be complicated. In fact, simplicity often makes it more effective. The key is to make it relatable, to tap into universal themes that resonate with your audience's deepest desires and fears.

We'll talk more about storytelling on Chapter 4.

Contrast: Why difference matters

Standing out is also about contrast. To make an impact, your brand needs to be different not just for the sake of being different, but in a way that sets you apart from your competitors. This contrast creates a psychological effect that makes your brand more memorable. The human brain works by categorizing and comparing, so when a brand presents itself as radically different from the rest, it occupies a unique space in the mind.

Take Tesla, for example. In a world where car manufacturers focused on incremental improvements—better mileage, more features—Tesla disrupted the market by offering something entirely different: an electric future. The contrast between Tesla and its gasoline-powered counterparts wasn't just technological; it was ideological. That difference was so stark, so bold, that it made Tesla impossible to ignore.

Repetition reinforces standing out

While novelty draws people in, repetition makes them stay. In branding, the concept of *mere exposure* suggests that the more often people see something, the more they like it. Familiarity breeds comfort, and comfort builds trust. The trick, however, is to balance novelty with repetition. Brands need to maintain their core message while finding fresh ways to deliver it.

This is why consistent branding is so important. From your logo to your messaging to your overall tone, consistency creates a sense of reliability. When customers see your brand repeatedly and in different contexts—ads, social media, products—it reinforces your presence in their minds. But it's not about being repetitive; it's about being consistently distinct.

The risk of blending in

The moment a brand starts to blend in, it's game over. The marketplace is full of brands that are "good enough" but lack any real distinction. These are the brands that get lost in the noise, that never quite manage to capture anyone's attention because they don't give the audience a reason to care. It's not enough to simply offer a quality product anymore—there needs to be something more, something that sets you apart.

One of the most common mistakes brands make is focusing too much on their competitors and not enough on their own identity. By constantly trying to match or beat the competition, they end up mimicking them, which only leads to more sameness. The key to standing out is to stop looking around and start looking inward—at what makes your brand truly unique.

Tapping into human psychology for success

The brands that understand the psychology of standing out are the ones that last. It's not about flashy campaigns or loud slogans—it's about tapping into the core of human nature. People notice what's different, they remember what moves them emotionally, and they trust what they see repeatedly.

In the end, standing out isn't a tactic—it's a strategy. And the brands that master it create more than just customers; they create movements, communities, and loyal advocates who can't help but spread the word.

The next step? Learning how to escape the commodity trap and make sure your brand never becomes just another option on the shelf. Stay tuned, because that's where the real transformation begins.

Escaping the commodity trap

The commodity trap is one of the deadliest places for a brand to be. It's where price wars, razor-thin margins, and constant discounting rule the day. In this trap, everything looks the same, and the only way to win is to be the cheapest option available. But here's the truth: you can't win on price alone. No one wins the race to the bottom.

Commodities are products or services that are indistinguishable from one another. Whether it's sugar, flour, or gasoline, the assumption is that all options are essentially the same. This mindset is fatal for brands because it strips away the power of differentiation and reduces everything to price. The moment your brand is seen as a commodity, your value is dictated not by what you offer but by how little you can charge for it.

Escaping the commodity trap is essential for survival. The good news? You can avoid it with a clear, compelling strategy that makes your brand stand out for reasons beyond price.

The commoditization of everything

At first glance, commoditization seems to be a problem that only affects low-margin, high-volume industries like agriculture or fuel. But look a little closer, and you'll see that commoditization can happen to any product, any industry—even luxury brands. When consumers perceive little to no difference between offerings, everything becomes a commodity. And that's when the race to the bottom begins.

Consider what's happened in the mobile phone market. For a long time, phones were increasingly seen as commodities—nearly every manufacturer was offering the same features, the same designs, with only small variations. Apple changed the game by refusing to play by those rules. Instead of competing on features or price, they created a brand around lifestyle, design, and innovation. People didn't buy iPhones just because of their specs—they bought them because owning an iPhone meant something. That's the difference between becoming a commodity and breaking free of the trap.

The danger of focusing only on price

Price is the most obvious lever to pull when things get tough. When sales dip, many companies reflexively cut prices, hoping to win over bargain-hunters. But while this might generate a short-term spike in sales, it's a losing strategy in the long run. Once you position yourself as the cheapest option, you've set an expectation that's nearly impossible to escape.

Walmart is an example of a company that thrives in the commodity space by dominating on price. But unless your business model is built specifically for this strategy, slashing prices just pushes you closer to becoming a commodity. When you compete on price alone, you're telling customers that price is your most important attribute, and if someone else comes along with a lower price, you'll lose.

Value trumps price

The key to escaping the commodity trap is to shift the focus from price to value. And value doesn't just mean offering more features for the same price—it's about creating an experience that's worth more in the eyes of the customer.

Consider Starbucks. Is their coffee significantly better than any other coffee you can get at a local café? Probably not. But what Starbucks does brilliantly is offer an experience: the ambiance, the customization, the sense of community. People are willing to pay more for a Starbucks latte because they're buying into an experience that's bigger than just the product. That's how you escape the commodity trap—by offering something so unique, so desirable, that people are willing to pay more for it.

Focus on differentiation, not competition

One of the biggest mistakes brands make is getting caught up in what their competitors are doing. The more you try to outdo the competition at their own game, the more you blend in. And once you blend in, you're just another option in the same category—a commodity.

The secret to escaping this trap is to stop playing by your competitors' rules. Instead of focusing on what everyone else is doing, double down on what makes you unique. Look at Dollar Shave Club. They entered a highly commoditized market—razors—and created a brand that wasn't about the product at all. They used humor, irreverence, and bold marketing to stand out in an industry dominated by giants like Gillette. Dollar Shave Club didn't compete on price (though they were affordable)—they competed on brand personality and convenience. And they won.

Personalization is power

Another strategy to avoid commoditization is to offer personalized experiences. When your brand makes people feel like they're getting something tailored specifically for them, they're far less likely to treat you as a commodity. Personalization makes your brand irreplaceable.

Consider Netflix, for instance. At its core, Netflix offers the same content as many other streaming services—movies, TV shows, documentaries. But what sets Netflix apart is its ability to curate and recommend content based on individual preferences. That level of personalization makes Netflix feel unique to each user, even though millions of people are watching the same shows. The experience feels tailored, and that's what keeps people subscribed.

Emotional differentiation

As we've explored in previous chapters, emotional differentiation is a powerful tool. Commodities are cold, impersonal, and interchangeable. But brands with emotional appeal? They can't be swapped out so easily. When people feel a personal connection to a brand, it becomes part of their identity, and no discount or price cut from a competitor can shake that loyalty.

Harley-Davidson is a masterclass in this kind of differentiation. Their motorcycles aren't commodities—they're symbols of freedom, rebellion, and independence. You don't buy a Harley just to get from point A to point B. You buy a Harley because it represents something deeper. That's the power of emotional differentiation—it builds bonds that transcend price.

Escaping requires courage

Breaking free from the commodity trap isn't easy. It requires courage—courage to resist the lure of short-term sales boosts through price cuts, courage to innovate, and courage to build a brand that stands for something more. It's about taking risks, but calculated ones. The rewards? Customers who choose your brand not because it's the cheapest, but because it's the only one that offers exactly what they need.

Ultimately, escaping the commodity trap is about reclaiming your identity and focusing on what makes your brand irreplaceable. It's about shifting the conversation from price to value, from product to experience, and from commodity to connection.

Next, we'll take a closer look at brands that have done this successfully—brands like Apple, Tesla, and Harley-Davidson. They've not only escaped the commodity trap; they've turned their differentiation into a competitive advantage that reshapes entire industries.

Case studies: Apple, Tesla, Harley-Davidson

Some brands don't just escape the commodity trap—they obliterate it. They go beyond merely standing out; they transform entire industries by creating a category of their own. Apple, Tesla, and Harley-Davidson are shining examples of brands that didn't settle for average. They forged unique identities that turned their products into cultural icons, not just commodities.

But how did they do it? What's the secret sauce that keeps these brands at the forefront of innovation, loyalty, and longevity? Let's break down their strategies and see how they mastered the art of differentiation.

Apple: Design, culture, and innovation

Apple is the poster child of differentiation. From its inception, Apple has never competed on price. In fact, its products are often among the most expensive in their categories. But Apple customers aren't paying for just a phone or computer—they're paying for an experience, an ideology, and a statement of identity.

When Apple launched its iconic "Think Different" campaign in 1997, it wasn't just selling computers. It was selling rebellion against the ordinary, an invitation to those who saw themselves as creative visionaries, innovators, and outsiders. Apple became the brand for those who *think differently*—the artists, the nonconformists, the dreamers. This identity allowed Apple to transcend the features-and-specs battle that most tech companies found themselves stuck in.

One of Apple's greatest strengths has been its focus on design. While other brands chased raw specifications—processor speed, memory, megapixels—Apple understood that form and function are inseparable. Its minimalist, intuitive designs created an emotional connection with users, turning everyday devices into objects of desire. An iPhone isn't just a phone; it's a status symbol, a reflection of personal style, and a tool for creativity.

Moreover, Apple built an ecosystem that fosters loyalty. Once you own one Apple product, you're drawn into a seamless experience across devices—from MacBooks to iPads to the Apple Watch. This interconnectedness keeps customers within the Apple family, making it difficult to switch to another brand. That level of emotional and functional loyalty is nearly impossible to replicate in a commodity-driven market.

Tesla: Revolutionizing an industry

Before Tesla, electric cars were a niche market—a curiosity for environmentally conscious consumers, but far from mainstream. Tesla didn't just enter the car market; it revolutionized it. Elon Musk's vision wasn't to sell electric cars as an alternative; it was to make them the future. And in doing so, Tesla turned the automotive industry on its head.

Tesla's differentiation is rooted in its bold mission: to accelerate the world's transition to sustainable energy. That's a lofty, world-changing ambition, and it's embedded in everything Tesla does. The company isn't just about selling cars—it's about shifting the entire narrative of transportation and energy consumption. This mission-driven approach resonates deeply with consumers who aren't just buying a car but are also buying into a movement.

But Tesla's differentiation goes beyond ideology. The company upended traditional business models in the car industry by cutting out dealerships and selling directly to consumers, which allowed for greater control over the customer experience. The technology behind Tesla's cars is also revolutionary. With constant software updates, over-the-air fixes, and cutting-edge autonomous driving features, Tesla positions itself as a tech company that happens to sell cars, rather than just another automaker.

Tesla also disrupted the luxury market by making electric cars desirable not just for environmental reasons but because they were fast, sleek, and aspirational. The Tesla Model S wasn't just an eco-friendly car—it was a luxury vehicle that could outperform many high-end gasoline cars. In this way, Tesla made it clear that choosing electric didn't mean sacrificing performance or style.

By combining innovation, mission, and design, Tesla transformed what could have been a commoditized product into something extraordinary.

Harley-Davidson: The power of identity

Few brands have mastered emotional differentiation as effectively as Harley-Davidson. This isn't just a motorcycle company; it's a brand that sells an identity—one rooted in freedom, rebellion, and rugged individuality.

Harley-Davidson's differentiation goes far beyond the mechanics of its bikes. The company's real power lies in the lifestyle it represents. Owning a Harley isn't just about transportation; it's about belonging to a tribe. The Harley-Davidson brand is wrapped up in the culture of the open road, leather jackets, and a distinct "badass" mentality. It appeals to those who don't want to blend in, who see themselves as rebels against the conformity of daily life.

This emotional connection has created a community of fiercely loyal customers. Harley owners don't just buy bikes—they buy into a culture. They join a tribe, attend rallies, and feel a deep sense of camaraderie with other Harley riders. That sense of belonging is what keeps people coming back to the brand, even when competitors offer bikes with more advanced technology or better specs.

Harley-Davidson's branding taps into a core human need: the desire to feel part of something bigger. The logo itself—bold, iconic, and instantly recognizable—has become a symbol of freedom, adventure, and independence. For many riders, owning a Harley isn't just a purchase; it's a rite of passage.

The lesson? Differentiation isn't about standing out for the sake of it—it's about creating a brand that people feel connected to, whether it's through design, ideology, or identity. These brands have taught us that in a world full of commodities, being unforgettable is the ultimate goal.

In the next chapter, we'll dive into some of the biggest myths surrounding uniqueness—and why being different *isn't* always the same as being meaningful.

CHAPTER 02

THE MYTHS OF UNIQUENESS

Gimmicks don't last

In the world of branding, it's easy to confuse "different" with "memorable." Brands often resort to gimmicks—flashy, temporary stunts designed to capture attention. But while a gimmick might buy you a moment of fame, it rarely builds lasting loyalty or respect. Gimmicks are like fireworks: they make a lot of noise, burn brightly for a second, and then vanish, leaving nothing behind but smoke.

The allure of the gimmick is strong. It's a quick fix, a way to stand out in the short term, especially in an era where consumers have limited attention spans. But the problem with relying on gimmicks is that they rarely offer substance. They might get people talking, but they don't give anyone a real reason to stick around once the initial excitement fades.

The danger of the short-term high

Brands that rely on gimmicks often find themselves in a cycle of diminishing returns. What starts as a buzz-worthy campaign ends up feeling hollow. Why? Because consumers are smarter than ever. They've learned to sniff out gimmicks, and when they do, they feel manipulated or let down. This creates a disconnect between the brand and the consumer, and once that trust is lost, it's hard to regain.

One infamous example of gimmick failure was Pepsi's "Kendall Jenner" ad. In an attempt to tap into the social justice movements that were gaining momentum, Pepsi created a commercial where Kendall Jenner "solved" a protest by handing a police officer a Pepsi. It was a classic case of a brand trying to leverage a serious social issue as a marketing tool without any real connection to the cause. The backlash was swift and brutal. Pepsi wasn't seen as an ally to the movement; it was seen as exploiting it for profit. The gimmick backfired, damaging the brand's credibility.

Gimmicks often appeal to a superficial sense of novelty, but they rarely build anything lasting. When brands rely on short-term stunts to make an impact, they risk losing sight of their long-term vision.

Authenticity over theatrics

In times where consumers crave authenticity, gimmicks are a risky game. People want brands to be real, transparent, and aligned with their values. Gimmicks, by nature, tend to feel contrived. They're designed to shock, amuse, or provoke, but they often lack the substance needed to build a meaningful connection.

Take the example of Snapchat's infamous "Spectacles" launch. The wearable glasses with built-in cameras were a playful, trendy idea, but ultimately, they felt more like a novelty than a game-changer. Despite the initial hype and limited-edition pop-up vending machines, the product didn't meet long-term needs, and sales dwindled. Snapchat had a brief moment of buzz, but it failed to turn that excitement into lasting value for its users.

In contrast, look at how Patagonia has avoided the gimmick trap by focusing on authenticity. Instead of flashy campaigns, Patagonia consistently reinforces its brand values around environmental activism. When they launched their "Don't Buy This Jacket" campaign, encouraging people to buy fewer products, it wasn't a stunt —it was a reflection of their deeply held belief in sustainability. The campaign worked because it was authentic, aligned with their mission, and didn't feel like a cheap trick to get attention.

Building trust takes time

One of the biggest mistakes brands make when they rely on gimmicks is assuming that attention equals loyalty. It doesn't. Loyalty is built over time, through consistent, meaningful interactions that reinforce a brand's core values and purpose. Gimmicks, on the other hand, are fleeting—they're designed to grab attention, but they rarely contribute to building long-term trust.

Red Bull is a great example of a brand that has avoided the gimmick trap while still pulling off bold, attention-grabbing campaigns. Yes, Red Bull is known for stunts—like sponsoring extreme sports events or even a man jumping from the edge of space —but these aren't gimmicks. They're part of the brand's DNA. Red Bull isn't just selling an energy drink; it's selling a lifestyle. The stunts they pull off align perfectly with their core message of pushing limits and living life to the extreme. There's substance behind the spectacle.

Compare this with brands that pull a one-time publicity stunt that has no connection to their identity. It might generate headlines for a day, but what does it leave behind? If your brand doesn't have a deeper story or a real mission driving it, consumers will quickly move on to the next flashy thing.

The long game: Substance over flash

Building a lasting brand means playing the long game. It means investing in a clear identity, staying true to your values, and creating a consistent narrative that resonates with your audience. Gimmicks might get people in the door, but they won't keep them around.

Consider the difference between a brand like IKEA and one like RadioShack. IKEA doesn't need to rely on gimmicks because it has built a solid foundation of trust over decades. Its brand promise — affordable, stylish, flat-pack furniture that's accessible to all — remains clear and consistent. RadioShack, on the other hand, became known for desperate, short-term marketing tactics, from Super Bowl ads to clearance sales, as it tried to stay relevant in a changing market. But because those tactics lacked depth, they weren't enough to save the brand from eventual collapse.

To escape the temptation of the gimmick, focus on your brand's core mission. Ask yourself: What are you really offering? Why should people care beyond the initial excitement? If the answers to these questions aren't clear, no amount of flashy stunts will save you.

The lasting impact of real differentiation

Real differentiation isn't about being loud — it's about being meaningful. It's about understanding who you are as a brand and what you stand for, and then communicating that in a way that connects deeply with your audience. Brands that stand the test of time don't rely on temporary thrills to stay relevant. They build strong foundations of trust, authenticity, and consistent value.

Apple didn't become a cultural icon because of a series of gimmicks. It became iconic because it consistently delivered on its promise to "Think Different." Harley-Davidson didn't capture the hearts of riders by pulling marketing stunts; it did so by creating an emotional connection that resonates with freedom, rebellion, and individuality.

The brands that thrive over the long term are the ones that move beyond superficial differentiation and focus on creating something real—something people can believe in.

So, the next time you're tempted by the quick win of a gimmick, remember: gimmicks don't last. Substance, authenticity, and a clear brand identity are the things that endure.

Next, we'll dive into *The danger of "good enough"* and why settling for adequacy is just as dangerous as relying on gimmicks.

The danger of "good enough"

"Good enough" is the enemy of greatness. It's tempting to think that just being adequate will get the job done, especially when your competitors aren't offering anything revolutionary. But in a market where consumers are constantly bombarded with choices, "good enough" is never enough. It might seem like a safe bet, but it's actually one of the most dangerous positions a brand can take.

The problem with being "good enough" is that it's forgettable. It's like blending into the background of a crowded room—nobody notices you, nobody remembers you, and ultimately, nobody cares. Brands that settle for "good enough" fail to inspire loyalty, fail to stand out, and eventually, fail to survive.

The comfort of mediocrity

Mediocrity feels safe. It's comfortable. After all, if you're not pushing boundaries, you're less likely to make mistakes or alienate anyone. You might even have a loyal customer base who's content with what you offer. But this false sense of security is precisely why brands that settle for "good enough" find themselves slipping into irrelevance.

The invisible threat of stagnation

When a brand settles for being "good enough," it usually means it has stopped innovating. Stagnation is an invisible threat—slow, creeping, and hard to notice until it's too late. It's like a slow leak in a tire. Everything seems fine at first, but eventually, your brand's performance falters, and by the time you realize what's happening, you're already trailing behind.

The marketplace is filled with companies that were once industry leaders but became complacent, only to be disrupted by more agile, forward-thinking competitors. Look at Blockbuster. For years, Blockbuster was the king of video rentals. Their model worked, their customers were satisfied, and they saw no reason to change. But as streaming technology developed, they failed to innovate. Netflix, which had started as a DVD rental-by-mail service, quickly pivoted to streaming and built a completely new entertainment ecosystem. Blockbuster's "good enough" approach left them blindsided by the future.

Consumer expectations evolve

The danger with "good enough" is that consumer expectations are constantly evolving. What might be acceptable today could be seen as outdated tomorrow. Brands that settle for adequacy are essentially putting themselves at the mercy of changing trends and innovations. By the time they realize they need to catch up, they've already lost their edge.

Think about the fast food industry. McDonald's, for decades, was the undisputed leader. But as consumer preferences shifted towards healthier, fresher options, McDonald's struggled to keep up. Meanwhile, newer chains like Chipotle, which emphasized customization and transparency in food sourcing, captured the attention of a health-conscious generation. McDonald's realized too late that "good enough" wasn't cutting it anymore, and they've been playing catch-up ever since.

Why "good enough" isn't memorable

One of the biggest dangers of "good enough" is that it isn't memorable. In a crowded marketplace, brands need to give people a reason to remember them. A reason to choose them over their competitors. But when your product, service, or brand message is just adequate, it doesn't leave a lasting impression.

Imagine going to a restaurant that serves decent food. You leave satisfied, but not wowed. There's nothing bad to say about the experience, but nothing particularly great either. The next time you're choosing where to eat, that restaurant doesn't come to mind because it was simply forgettable. The same is true for brands. If you're not delivering something remarkable—something worth talking about—people will forget you the moment a better option comes along.

The cost of playing it safe

Consumers have more choices than ever before. If your brand doesn't offer something compelling, if it doesn't inspire, excite, or resonate on a deeper level, your customers will quickly move on to a brand that does. Loyalty is fragile, and in the end, the cost of being "good enough" is losing the very customers you thought you were keeping safe.

Breaking free from "good enough"

So, how do brands break free from the trap of mediocrity? It starts with a mindset shift. Being remarkable requires a willingness to take risks, to innovate, and to push beyond what feels safe. It means consistently asking, "How can we do better?" rather than, "Is this good enough?"

Breaking free from "good enough" also requires a deep understanding of your audience. What do they truly need? What do they value most? Brands that push beyond adequacy are the ones that anticipate and exceed consumer expectations, constantly evolving to meet changing demands.

The choice: "Good enough" or unforgettable?

At the end of the day, brands have a choice: settle for being "good enough" and risk blending into the background, or strive for greatness and stand out in a sea of mediocrity. The brands that choose greatness — the ones that refuse to settle — are the ones that become unforgettable.

What's next? Are you just background noise? The following section will explore how brands can unintentionally fade into irrelevance by doing nothing remarkable. Don't miss it.

Are you just background noise?

In the chaos of today's marketplace, many brands unknowingly fall into the trap of becoming background noise. They're there, but no one really notices them. Like a dull hum in the distance, they fade into irrelevance, blending into the sea of sameness that surrounds them.

The biggest mistake brands make is assuming that visibility alone is enough. Just because your brand exists in the marketplace doesn't mean people are paying attention. In fact, without a clear point of differentiation, your brand becomes part of the clutter — another option among endless alternatives.

The illusion of presence

Being present doesn't guarantee being seen. Many brands spend enormous budgets on marketing, advertising, and social media to stay in front of consumers. But the truth is, without something compelling to say, you're just adding to the noise. Consumers have become adept at tuning out anything that doesn't grab them immediately, which means a forgettable brand message is worse than no message at all.

Remember Yahoo? In the early 2000s, Yahoo was everywhere—search engines, email, news. Yet, they failed to evolve, and while they remained "visible," they became irrelevant as Google rose to dominate. Yahoo never found a unique voice or offering that set them apart, and today, they're a shadow of what they once were.

The danger of playing it safe

Many brands become background noise because they play it too safe. They don't want to take risks, so they settle for doing what everyone else is doing, hoping to blend in just enough to stay afloat. But blending in is the first step to disappearing.

Consider how the fast-food industry is filled with brands that offer the same menus, promotions, and marketing strategies. It's the innovators—like Chick-fil-A or Shake Shack—that stand out by offering something different, whether it's exceptional customer service, healthier options, or a unique dining experience. Playing it safe might feel secure, but it often leads to mediocrity.

Consistency vs. monotony

While consistency is key to building trust, monotony is what happens when a brand becomes predictable. If your audience can guess your next move, you're in danger of losing them. Consistency should reflect your brand's values, but there must be room for evolution and excitement.

Take a look at brands like Netflix. They remain consistent in their mission to deliver quality content, but they keep things fresh by constantly innovating with original programming, global content, and interactive features. They aren't just another streaming service—they're constantly redefining what entertainment can be.

Stand for something or stand aside

A sure way to avoid becoming background noise is to stand for something meaningful. Brands with a clear purpose or cause resonate more deeply with consumers. Patagonia is a prime example of a brand that refuses to fade into the background. They don't just sell outdoor gear—they advocate for environmental causes, which gives them a powerful voice and a loyal following. When your brand stands for something greater than the product itself, you move from background noise to the center of attention.

The cost of being forgettable

In a crowded market, forgettable brands are the first to disappear. People don't talk about you, they don't remember you, and they certainly don't stay loyal to you. It's not enough to be adequate—you have to be remarkable. If you're not giving consumers a reason to care, you've already lost them.

The path forward is clear: don't be content with just being another option. Strive to be the only option that truly matters to your audience.

Next up: we'll explore how some of the most iconic brands fell into irrelevance—and what they could have done differently to avoid being just background noise.

Brands that didn't make it

Not every brand survives the test of time. Some fade into obscurity not because they lacked resources, but because they failed to adapt, innovate, or differentiate. The graveyard of once-prominent brands is full of cautionary tales—brands that had the spotlight but couldn't hold onto it.

Failure often comes down to a simple truth: when a brand stops offering something unique, it becomes forgettable. And forgettable brands eventually disappear.

Blockbuster: A failure to evolve

Blockbuster's demise is one of the most famous examples of a brand that couldn't keep up with change. At its peak, Blockbuster dominated the video rental market. Thousands of stores across the world made the brand nearly synonymous with movie nights.

But as technology evolved, Blockbuster clung to its physical stores while companies like Netflix embraced the digital future. Netflix didn't just compete; it changed the rules of the game, offering streaming services that rendered video rentals obsolete. Blockbuster had the opportunity to innovate but stayed locked in a business model that was rapidly becoming outdated.

The lesson here? Innovation isn't optional. The market never stops moving, and brands that don't evolve with it quickly find themselves left behind.

Toys "R" Us: Ignoring customer shifts

For decades, Toys "R" Us was the go-to destination for children's toys. The giant giraffe mascot and endless aisles of toys were an icon of childhood for many. However, as online retail rose and consumer behavior shifted, Toys "R" Us struggled to adapt. They were slow to invest in e-commerce and ignored the convenience of shopping on Amazon and other online platforms. By the time they tried to pivot, it was too late.

The collapse of Toys "R" Us wasn't just about competition from online retailers. The brand also lost touch with how modern consumers shop for and buy toys. Customers weren't looking for just a warehouse of toys anymore—they wanted a more curated, personalized shopping experience, something Toys "R" Us didn't offer.

Being big isn't enough if you're not paying attention to where your customers are going.

Nokia: From leader to laggard

Nokia once held nearly 50% of the global mobile phone market. They were the leader in mobile communication, known for their durable phones and cutting-edge technology. Yet, when smartphones emerged, Nokia failed to pivot fast enough. They underestimated the impact of the iPhone and continued to focus on traditional handsets long after it was clear the market was shifting.

While Apple and Samsung were revolutionizing how people interacted with their devices, Nokia clung to what had worked in the past. The company tried to catch up, but by then, they were playing a losing game. In the end, their failure to foresee the smartphone revolution turned Nokia from an industry leader into a cautionary tale.

Sears: The cost of complacency

Sears, once one of the largest retailers in America, is another brand that crumbled under the weight of its own complacency. The company had been a retail giant for over a century, with everything from household goods to clothing under one roof. But instead of innovating alongside the rise of e-commerce, Sears stuck to its outdated business model.

Amazon and Walmart adapted to online shopping trends, while Sears seemed stuck in the past. What Sears failed to realize was that simply being a big name wasn't enough. The rise of digital shopping required a complete rethinking of how retail operated, and Sears was too slow to react. Their stores began closing, one by one, until the brand was all but erased from relevance.

Kodak: Missing the digital wave

Kodak's story is perhaps one of the most ironic in the world of business failures. The company actually invented the digital camera, but instead of embracing the new technology, Kodak buried it, fearing it would cannibalize their film business. In trying to protect their legacy, Kodak ignored the future of photography.

As digital cameras gained popularity and smartphones integrated high-quality cameras, Kodak's film business dwindled. They could have been the leader of the digital revolution, but instead, they clung to a dying industry. By the time they tried to pivot, it was too late.

Kodak's downfall serves as a reminder that being attached to the past can prevent a brand from seizing the future.

The price of missing the moment

These brands didn't fail because they were small or underfunded. They failed because they missed their moment to adapt. In each case, a combination of complacency, failure to innovate, and not listening to shifting consumer needs sealed their fate.

The takeaway is clear: no brand, no matter how big or iconic, is immune to becoming obsolete. The market rewards those who evolve, who take risks, and who never stop pushing forward.

Next, we'll explore how to create a *real* Unique Value Proposition—one that cuts through the noise and gives your brand a lasting edge.

CHAPTER 03

CRAFTING A UNIQUE VALUE PROPOSITION

Beyond buzzwords: Real USP

If you work in marketing, you know buzzwords get thrown around like confetti. You'll hear terms like "disruptive," "innovative," and "cutting-edge" attached to everything from toothpaste to tech startups. But here's the truth: buzzwords don't sell. What does sell is a clear, genuine, and compelling Unique Selling Proposition (USP). A real USP isn't just a catchy phrase or an industry cliché—it's the essence of what sets your brand apart in a way that matters to your customers.

Too many brands lean on buzzwords because they sound impressive, but without substance, they become empty noise. Consumers today are smart, and they see right through vague promises. A real USP goes beyond the trendy terms and speaks to a core truth about your brand—one that no one else can claim.

What a USP really is

At its core, a USP is your brand's distinct value. It answers a simple but critical question: *Why should a customer choose you over your competitors?*

But crafting a real USP is harder than it sounds. It's not enough to say you're "better" or "faster" than the competition. A strong USP digs deeper, offering a unique promise that resonates with your target audience's specific needs, desires, or problems. It's about solving a problem in a way that no one else can, or giving customers a benefit they can't get anywhere else.

Take Domino's Pizza, for example. When they launched their now-famous USP—"You get fresh, hot pizza delivered to your door in 30 minutes or less, or it's free"—it wasn't about being the best pizza in the world. Domino's didn't promise to out-cook gourmet pizzerias. Instead, they leaned into a value proposition that mattered to their customers: speed. At the time, quick delivery was a differentiator, and that bold guarantee set Domino's apart.

Moving beyond meaningless buzzwords

The problem with buzzwords is they're overused and underdelivered. Everyone claims to be "innovative" or "customer-centric," but how many brands actually follow through on those promises? If your USP relies on overused phrases without backing them up with real value, you're doing more harm than good.

Consider the tech industry. Every company claims to be "disruptive," but how many are truly changing the game? Real disruption comes from brands like Tesla, which didn't just promise to revolutionize the car industry—they did it. Tesla's USP isn't a buzzword; it's a commitment to redefining what cars can be, rooted in a mission to accelerate the world's transition to sustainable energy. They didn't settle for vague language—they built their USP around a vision that's clear, specific, and revolutionary.

The dangers of trying to appeal to everyone

A real USP is focused, not broad. Trying to appeal to everyone usually results in a generic message that doesn't resonate with anyone. The most successful brands know who they're for—and, just as importantly, who they're *not* for.

Think about Harley-Davidson. Their USP is about more than selling motorcycles—it's about selling freedom, rebellion, and a lifestyle. Harley isn't trying to be all things to all people. They know that their message won't resonate with everyone, and that's okay. By focusing on a specific audience, Harley-Davidson creates a stronger emotional connection with the people who matter most to their brand. That's the power of a focused USP.

Finding your true USP

Finding a real USP requires asking the tough questions: *What do we do better than anyone else? What can we offer that no one else can? What problem do we solve for our customers that makes their lives better?* Answering these questions requires a deep understanding of your strengths and your audience's needs.

A strong USP can't just be a marketing slogan. It has to be embedded in everything your brand does. From your products to your customer service to your marketing campaigns, your USP should be reflected at every touchpoint.

For example, Warby Parker's USP isn't just about affordable eyewear. They positioned themselves as a company that offers stylish, high-quality glasses at a fraction of the price you'd pay at traditional retailers. But their USP goes deeper—they've also built a reputation for exceptional customer service and a socially responsible business model, giving a pair of glasses to someone in need for every pair purchased. Warby Parker's USP isn't a buzzword; it's a clear promise that resonates with a specific customer base.

Evolving your USP

Your USP isn't static. As markets change and consumer needs evolve, so should your value proposition. A great example is Nike. Their original USP was all about high-performance athletic gear. But over time, Nike has evolved into something much bigger. Today, Nike isn't just selling shoes—they're selling a mindset. Their "Just Do It" campaign taps into a deeper emotional appeal, encouraging athletes of all levels to push beyond their limits. Nike's USP now speaks to empowerment and personal achievement, which has allowed them to stay relevant across generations.

Making your USP stick

Once you've identified your USP, the next step is making sure it sticks. Your USP should be the backbone of your entire brand strategy, guiding how you communicate with your audience, how you position your products, and how you approach every customer interaction.

To make it truly effective, your USP needs to be consistent across all channels. Whether a customer sees your message on social media, in-store, or through an email, the core promise of your brand should be clear and unmistakable. Consistency builds trust, and trust builds loyalty.

Ultimately, a strong USP isn't about flashy language or empty promises. It's about delivering real, tangible value in a way that no one else can. When you go beyond the buzzwords, you give your customers a reason to choose you—and to stick with you.

In the next section, we'll explore how to find your true audience—the people who will respond to your USP and become your most loyal customers.

Find your true audience

Your brand isn't for everyone, and that's a good thing. Trying to appeal to a broad, generic audience is a surefire way to dilute your message and lose relevance. The key to building a strong, differentiated brand is knowing *exactly* who you're speaking to and why they care.

Finding your true audience isn't about casting the widest net—it's about casting the *right* net. It's about narrowing down the people who resonate with your brand's message, values, and products, and focusing all your efforts on speaking directly to them. When you know who you're for, everything else falls into place.

The myth of mass appeal

Many brands fall into the trap of believing they need to please everyone to grow. The idea of mass appeal is tempting—after all, shouldn't you want as many customers as possible? But when you try to appeal to everyone, you risk becoming watered down and forgettable. Brands with a broad message often struggle to form a real connection with anyone because they aren't speaking clearly to any specific group.

Think of Apple versus Microsoft in the early 2000s. While Microsoft dominated the corporate market, Apple carved out a clear niche—creatives, artists, and forward-thinkers. Apple didn't try to be everything to everyone. Instead, they zeroed in on people who aligned with their "Think Different" philosophy, and that clarity is what made Apple a cultural phenomenon. They built deep loyalty by knowing who they were for, not by trying to serve everyone.

The power of a defined audience

Brands that know their audience can make stronger, more authentic connections. This happens because they understand not just what their customers need, but *who* they are. When you understand your audience on a deeper level—what drives them, what they value, what they struggle with—you can speak to them in a way that feels personal and relevant.

Consider Glossier, a brand that revolutionized the beauty industry by catering to a very specific audience: young women who value a minimalist, effortless approach to beauty. Glossier didn't waste time trying to compete with the heavyweights of the cosmetics industry. Instead, they honed in on their target—customers who wanted simple, clean beauty products—and created a community around that vision. By knowing their audience inside and out, they created a cult-like following and became a standout brand in an otherwise crowded market.

Avoiding the trap of broad messaging

To find your true audience, you need to avoid the trap of broad, generic messaging. A message that tries to speak to everyone will resonate with no one. You have to be willing to be specific—even if that means alienating some people. A focused message allows you to connect deeply with the right people, rather than skimming the surface with the masses.

Take Patagonia, for instance. They don't try to appeal to everyone who might need outdoor gear. They're laser-focused on customers who care about the environment and sustainability, and they make it clear in every facet of their business. Their products, marketing, and even activism speak directly to this audience, and it's helped them create a community that's deeply loyal and fiercely protective of the brand. Patagonia's commitment to their audience goes beyond products—it's a shared set of values.

How to define your audience

Defining your true audience requires going beyond demographics like age, gender, or location. It's about understanding the psychographics—what motivates your audience, what their challenges are, and what values they hold dear. This is where real brand differentiation happens: when you understand not just *who* your audience is, but *why* they make the choices they do.

Start by asking these questions:

- What problem are we solving, and who has that problem?
- What are the values and beliefs of our ideal customers?
- What does our audience care about beyond just the product?

Answering these questions helps you craft messaging and products that speak to the heart of your audience. It's not about guessing; it's about truly understanding who your brand is for and aligning everything you do with that group.

Embrace exclusivity

Knowing your audience means embracing the idea that your brand isn't for everyone—and that's a powerful position to be in. When you cater to a specific group, you create a sense of exclusivity. Your audience feels like they're part of something special, something that reflects their unique tastes, needs, or values.

Brands like Supreme have mastered this. Supreme isn't trying to sell to everyone who wants streetwear—they've built a brand that appeals to a very specific audience of hypebeasts, fashion enthusiasts, and trendsetters. Their limited drops and high-demand products create a sense of scarcity and exclusivity, which strengthens the loyalty and devotion of their audience.

When you find your true audience, it's no longer about chasing customers. It's about attracting the right ones—those who believe in what you stand for and are willing to stick with you through the long haul.

The long-term value of knowing your audience

Brands that know their true audience don't just create customers; they create advocates. When people feel that a brand speaks to them on a personal level, they become more than buyers—they become loyal supporters who spread the word, bring in new customers, and defend the brand fiercely. This kind of loyalty is invaluable, and it's built through a deep understanding of who your audience is and what matters to them.

The challenge isn't just finding your true audience—it's staying committed to them. As your brand grows, it can be tempting to widen your reach and dilute your message to appeal to more people. But brands that maintain a clear focus on their core audience tend to have more lasting power.

Next, we'll dive into understanding what your brand is really selling—and why your true offering is often much deeper than just the product on the shelf.

What are you really selling?

Brands often make the mistake of focusing too much on the product itself. They talk about features, benefits, and technical specifications, assuming that's what will win over customers. But the truth is, people don't just buy products—they buy feelings, solutions, and stories. The real value of your brand lies in what it represents, the experience it delivers, and the emotional connection it creates.

If your brand is focused solely on the product, you're missing out on the bigger picture. What you're really selling is often much deeper than the physical object or service you offer. It's the transformation, the identity, or the problem you solve that resonates most with your audience.

Selling the transformation

One of the most powerful things a brand can do is sell the transformation that comes from using its product or service. People don't just want a product—they want the outcome it promises. Nike, for example, doesn't just sell athletic gear. They sell the promise of achievement, of pushing past limits and unlocking your inner athlete. Their marketing isn't about shoes or shirts; it's about what happens when you *just do it*.

Understanding the transformation your product offers is key to elevating your brand. Are you making life easier, saving time, or helping customers become the person they aspire to be? By focusing on the transformation rather than the features, you create a deeper connection with your audience.

The emotional value

People buy on emotion and justify with logic. This is a basic principle of consumer behavior. The features of a product might appeal to logic, but emotions are what drive purchasing decisions. Apple understands this better than anyone. While they certainly offer top-notch technology, what they really sell is creativity, self-expression, and innovation. Owning an Apple device is about more than just having a tool—it's about aligning with a brand that stands for individuality and thinking differently.

When you tap into the emotional value of your brand, you go beyond selling a product. You're selling a feeling, a sense of belonging, or an aspirational identity. Brands like Harley-Davidson don't sell motorcycles—they sell freedom, rebellion, and the open road. That emotional connection is why Harley riders are some of the most loyal customers in the world.

Solving the deeper problem

It's easy to think of your brand as selling a solution to a straightforward problem. But if you dig deeper, you'll often find that the problem your customers are trying to solve is more complex than it appears. Starbucks, for example, doesn't just sell coffee. They sell a place of comfort, a familiar ritual, and a sense of community. For many, Starbucks is a third place — neither home nor work — where they can feel connected or take a break from the chaos of their day.

What problem are you solving that goes beyond the obvious? Are you providing convenience in a hectic world? A sense of identity in a crowded marketplace? Or perhaps you're offering reassurance in times of uncertainty? The more you understand the deeper needs of your audience, the more effective your messaging and branding will be.

The story behind the product

Your product is part of a larger narrative, and that story can be more powerful than the product itself. When a customer buys from your brand, they're often buying into a story — a set of values, a mission, or a purpose that aligns with their own.

Consider Patagonia. They sell high-quality outdoor gear, but what customers are really buying into is the brand's commitment to environmental sustainability. Patagonia's story is one of activism and responsibility, and that story is woven into every product they sell. Their customers aren't just buying jackets; they're buying into a movement that aligns with their values.

Every brand has a story, whether it's about the founder's journey, the mission behind the product, or the values that drive the company. When you embrace that story, you give customers something to believe in — something more meaningful than the product itself.

Selling experiences, not things

People remember experiences more than they remember products. This is why many of the world's most successful brands focus on delivering exceptional customer experiences. Take Disney, for example. They aren't just selling theme park tickets or movie merchandise — they're selling magic. The Disney experience is carefully crafted to transport people into a world of imagination and wonder, and that's what keeps customers coming back, generation after generation.

Experiences create lasting memories and emotional connections. Whether it's an unforgettable unboxing experience, superior customer service, or a seamless online shopping experience, brands that focus on selling experiences rather than just products stand out.

Going beyond the transaction

The most successful brands understand that they aren't just selling a product—they're selling a relationship. Every interaction with your brand, from customer service to marketing to the post-purchase experience, is part of the larger picture. A real brand experience doesn't end when the customer buys your product—it's just beginning.

Building a relationship means creating trust, offering consistent value, and staying relevant to your customer's evolving needs. Brands like Amazon have mastered this by focusing not just on what they sell, but on how they sell it. Their relentless focus on customer convenience—from fast shipping to easy returns—keeps customers loyal and coming back for more.

What are you really selling?

At its core, your brand is selling much more than the product on the shelf. You're selling an idea, an emotion, and a transformation. The brands that understand this create deeper connections with their customers, driving loyalty and long-term success.

Next, we'll explore how to craft a USP that truly resonates with your audience, so you can start selling more than just products—you can start selling meaning.

How to craft a resonating USP

A Unique Selling Proposition (USP) is more than just a clever slogan or a catchy tagline. It's the foundation of your brand's promise to its customers. But crafting a USP that truly resonates requires a deep understanding of both your brand and your audience. It needs to hit that sweet spot where what you offer perfectly aligns with what your customers value most.

A great USP should cut through the noise, provide clarity, and offer a compelling reason for customers to choose you over anyone else. But how do you create one that sticks? Let's break it down.

Know your audience inside out

The first step to crafting a resonating USP is understanding who you're speaking to. You need to know not just their demographics—age, gender, income—but their deeper motivations, desires, and pain points. What are their problems? What are their values? Why do they need your product or service in their life?

When you know your audience on this deeper level, you can craft a USP that speaks directly to their needs. Glossier, for instance, built its USP around real people who wanted simple, effective skincare solutions. By focusing on a specific audience—young women who value natural beauty and minimalism—they created a message that was more than skin deep.

Highlight what makes you different

Your USP should clearly articulate what sets you apart from the competition. This isn't just about being better—it's about being different in a way that matters to your customers. What can you do that no one else can? What unique advantage do you offer?

Consider FedEx's classic USP: "When it absolutely, positively has to be there overnight." This statement didn't just highlight their speed; it tapped into a key customer need—reliability. FedEx wasn't just selling delivery; they were selling peace of mind. By focusing on something their competitors couldn't guarantee, they became the go-to brand for time-sensitive shipments.

Simplify your message

Simplicity is the key to a powerful USP. Too many brands over-complicate their message, trying to pack in too much information or too many promises. The best USPs are clear, concise, and easy to remember. They get to the point, focusing on a single, compelling benefit that matters most to the customer.

Think about M&Ms: "Melts in your mouth, not in your hand." It's simple, direct, and memorable. The message is clear, and the benefit is specific. By boiling your USP down to its most essential element, you make it easier for customers to understand why they should choose you.

Focus on emotional resonance

A truly resonating USP doesn't just appeal to logic; it taps into emotion. People don't always make decisions based on facts and features—they make decisions based on how a brand makes them feel. Your USP should evoke an emotional response, whether it's excitement, trust, or a sense of belonging.

Take Nike's "Just Do It." It's not about the shoes; it's about the drive to push your limits and achieve greatness. That emotional appeal resonates with athletes of all levels and has made Nike one of the most iconic brands in the world. When crafting your USP, think about the emotional impact you want to have on your audience.

Be specific and bold

Vagueness is the death of a strong USP. Phrases like "high quality" or "great service" don't mean anything unless you back them up with specifics. A powerful USP is bold and confident, offering a specific promise that customers can rely on.

Domino's Pizza built its brand with the bold claim: "You get fresh, hot pizza delivered to your door in 30 minutes or less—or it's free." It's a clear, specific promise that customers could count on. That level of boldness not only made them stand out but also built trust with their customers.

Test and evolve

Once you've crafted your USP, it's important to test it. Does it resonate with your target audience? Does it make people take notice? If your USP isn't getting the reaction you want, don't be afraid to tweak it. Your USP should evolve with your brand and your audience, adapting to new challenges and opportunities.

Look at how brands like Starbucks have evolved their USP over time. Initially, Starbucks focused on premium coffee as its main differentiator. But as the market shifted, they expanded their USP to focus on the entire experience of their coffeehouses—the atmosphere, the community, and the personalized service. By evolving their USP, Starbucks has stayed relevant and continued to grow.

Align with your brand's core values

Your USP should be a reflection of your brand's core values. It's not just about what you sell, but why you sell it. A USP that aligns with your values will feel authentic, and that authenticity will resonate with your audience.

Take Patagonia as an example. Their USP is centered around sustainability and environmental responsibility: "We're in business to save our home planet." This isn't just a marketing angle—it's a reflection of their brand's mission and values. And because their USP is so deeply rooted in what they stand for, it resonates powerfully with their environmentally conscious audience.

Crafting your brand's legacy

A resonating USP isn't just a tool for today—it's a long-term asset that defines your brand's place in the market. When done right, your USP will guide everything from your product development to your marketing strategy, shaping how your brand is perceived and remembered.

So ask yourself: What's the one thing you can promise that no one else can? What's the unique value you bring to your customers' lives? Answer those questions, and you'll have the foundation for a USP that not only resonates but endures.

Next, we'll dive into understanding the emotional edge of branding—why winning hearts can often be more important than winning minds.

CHAPTER 04

THE EMOTIONAL EDGE

Winning hearts, not minds

In the battle for brand loyalty, logic rarely wins. Consumers may compare features, prices, and benefits, but what drives them to choose one brand over another often comes down to something far more powerful: emotion. Winning hearts is about creating an emotional connection that goes beyond rational thinking. It's about building a brand that resonates deeply with people, making them feel something—whether it's excitement, trust, or belonging.

While data and facts have their place, brands that rely solely on logic often struggle to stand out. People are emotional creatures, and the brands they connect with most are the ones that speak to their hearts.

The science of emotional decision-making

Decades of research in psychology and neuroscience show that people make decisions based on emotion first and then use logic to justify those choices. In fact, studies have shown that emotions play a critical role in our ability to make decisions at all. When we feel connected to a brand, it triggers emotional responses that override pure logic.

Think of Apple, a brand that consistently wins hearts before minds. Apple products aren't necessarily the most affordable or even the most technically superior. But the way Apple presents itself—through sleek design, innovative storytelling, and a focus on creativity—creates an emotional connection with its audience. Owning an Apple device is about being part of a community of forward-thinkers and innovators. Apple's success isn't built on specs; it's built on emotional appeal.

The power of brand storytelling

At the heart of emotional branding is storytelling. Great stories tap into our emotions, drawing us in and making us care. When a brand can tell a compelling story, it creates a sense of meaning and purpose that goes beyond the product itself.

Consider Nike's "Just Do It" campaign. The message is simple, but it's backed by powerful storytelling. Nike's ads aren't just about shoes; they're about athletes overcoming obstacles, pushing their limits, and achieving greatness. The emotional pull of these stories resonates deeply with Nike's audience, creating a bond that goes far beyond footwear. Nike isn't just selling products—they're selling inspiration and empowerment.

Storytelling helps brands connect with people on a personal level. It's not just about what your brand does, but why it matters. People want to feel like they're part of something bigger, and a well-told brand story gives them that opportunity.

Why emotional loyalty lasts longer

Loyalty built on emotion is far more resilient than loyalty based on logic. If someone chooses your brand solely because of a feature or a price point, they'll jump ship the moment a competitor offers something better or cheaper. But if you've captured their heart—if your brand makes them feel something—they're much more likely to stick with you, even in the face of better offers.

Harley-Davidson -again- is a perfect example of a brand that has mastered emotional loyalty. Harley riders don't just buy motorcycles—they buy a lifestyle, a sense of freedom and rebellion. That emotional connection is why Harley-Davidson has some of the most fiercely loyal customers in the world. They aren't just buying bikes; they're buying an identity.

Trust and emotional connection

Trust is another critical component of winning hearts. When consumers trust a brand, they feel safe, understood, and valued. Trust is built over time through consistent actions, transparency, and authenticity. Brands that foster trust through emotional connections are more likely to win long-term loyalty.

Look at Patagonia, a brand that has won the trust of its audience by being authentically committed to environmental causes. Customers trust Patagonia not just because of the quality of their products, but because they believe in the company's mission. Patagonia's emotional connection with its audience is rooted in shared values, and that trust keeps customers coming back, even when other outdoor brands may offer similar products.

Humanizing your brand

One of the best ways to create an emotional connection is by humanizing your brand. People connect with people, not faceless corporations. Brands that show vulnerability, personality, and a sense of humor often find it easier to win hearts. Being relatable and human in your communication can make a world of difference in how people perceive your brand.

Take Wendy's, for example. The fast-food chain has built an emotional connection with its audience by using a playful, witty, and sometimes even sarcastic tone on social media. Their interactions feel personal, fun, and authentic, which has made Wendy's a favorite on platforms like Twitter. Wendy's isn't just a brand selling burgers—they've become a personality that people enjoy interacting with.

Designing for emotion

It's not just what you say, but how you say it. Design plays a major role in creating an emotional connection. Whether it's the look and feel of your product, your website, or your packaging, every element should contribute to the emotional experience. The way your brand looks and feels can evoke specific emotions—excitement, comfort, nostalgia—that help create a deeper connection with your audience.

Take Disney, a master of designing for emotion. Everything from the iconic Disney logo to the immersive experiences in their theme parks is carefully crafted to evoke a sense of wonder, joy, and nostalgia. Disney's design isn't just functional—it's emotional, and it's that emotional impact that has made Disney a beloved brand for generations.

The risks of ignoring emotion

Brands that ignore the emotional side of consumer behavior risk becoming commodities. If your product is only selling based on features or price, you're leaving yourself vulnerable to being replaced the moment someone else offers a better deal. In contrast, brands that connect emotionally with their audience build a protective moat around themselves, making it harder for competitors to steal their customers.

Brands like Coca-Cola understand this well. Coca-Cola isn't just selling soda—it's selling happiness, sharing, and togetherness. Their messaging focuses on the emotional moments of joy and connection that come with sharing a Coke, which makes them much more than just a beverage brand. It's this emotional branding that has helped Coca-Cola maintain its global dominance for so long.

Winning hearts for the long run

Winning hearts isn't about short-term wins or one-off campaigns — it's about building a long-term emotional connection with your audience. The brands that understand this create lasting loyalty, turning customers into advocates who stick with them through thick and thin.

As we move forward, we'll dive deeper into how iconic brands use the power of emotional branding and storytelling to create loyal followings. Next up: we'll look at *The psychology of iconic brands* and how they master the art of emotional connection.

The psychology of iconic brands

What makes a brand iconic? It's not just about market share or being well-known. Iconic brands have a unique power: they create a lasting psychological and emotional impact on their audience. They aren't just products on a shelf; they become symbols, cultural touchstones, and a part of their customers' identities.

The most successful brands understand that to become iconic, they need to tap into deeper psychological forces. It's about creating meaning, telling a story, and building an emotional bond that goes far beyond the product itself. Iconic brands resonate with people on a visceral level, and that's why they stand the test of time.

The power of meaning

At the core of every iconic brand is a sense of meaning. These brands stand for something larger than the product they sell. It could be a mission, a set of values, or an idea that connects with their audience on an emotional and psychological level.

Take TOMS, for example. The brand didn't just sell shoes—they sold the idea of giving back. TOMS' "One for One" campaign, where they donated a pair of shoes for every pair purchased, became the brand's defining purpose. This mission resonated deeply with consumers who wanted to make a positive impact with their purchases. TOMS didn't just sell footwear; they sold a vision of making the world a better place, and that gave the brand lasting meaning.

When a brand stands for something, it gives customers a reason to feel proud of their connection to it. People want to align with brands that reflect their own values, and when they find one, they become loyal advocates.

Identity and self-expression

Iconic brands help people express who they are or who they want to be. They offer more than just a product—they offer a way for consumers to signal their identity, values, or lifestyle to the world. This is where the psychology of self-expression comes into play.

Take a brand like Jeep. Jeep isn't just selling vehicles—they're selling adventure, ruggedness, and an outdoor lifestyle. Owning a Jeep is a way for customers to identify themselves as explorers, people who are ready to tackle anything the road throws at them. It's not just transportation; it's a symbol of independence and adventure. That identity becomes a key part of why Jeep owners feel so connected to the brand.

The same principle applies to many fashion brands. Think about how people use clothing to express themselves. A brand like Levi's doesn't just sell jeans—they sell a timeless sense of style and authenticity. Wearing Levi's is about aligning with a brand that represents heritage, simplicity, and a laid-back lifestyle. Iconic fashion brands, like Levi's or Ralph Lauren, are able to tap into their customers' desire for self-expression, making their products much more than just clothes.

Consistency and reliability

One of the key psychological factors behind an iconic brand is consistency. These brands don't change their core message or values with every new trend—they remain true to who they are, which creates a sense of reliability and trust with their audience. Customers know exactly what they can expect when they engage with the brand, and that dependability builds lasting loyalty.

Coca-Cola is a perfect example of consistency in action. For decades, Coca-Cola has focused on themes of happiness, sharing, and togetherness. They haven't wavered from this core message, and as a result, consumers have a clear emotional connection to the brand that has been reinforced over generations. Coca-Cola represents more than just a drink—it's part of the fabric of family gatherings, celebrations, and moments of joy.

Cultural relevance

Iconic brands stay relevant by tapping into the culture of their time. They don't just follow trends—they influence them. These brands become part of the cultural conversation, often aligning with movements, shifts in society, or generational changes.

Look at Nike's "Dream Crazy" campaign, which featured Colin Kaepernick. By aligning themselves with social justice movements and standing up for what they believed in, Nike tapped into a cultural moment that resonated with a large segment of their audience. This wasn't just about selling shoes—it was about Nike positioning itself as a brand that supports boldness, courage, and fighting for change. Nike's cultural relevance made the brand iconic for a new generation of consumers.

Brands that are culturally aware and willing to take a stand—whether it's about social issues, environmental concerns, or lifestyle changes—can create deeper connections with their audience. They become more than just companies; they become part of the cultural zeitgeist.

The psychology of nostalgia

Iconic brands often play on the power of nostalgia. Tapping into the past can evoke powerful emotional responses, reminding people of simpler, happier times. This psychological trigger helps brands maintain a sense of familiarity and comfort, even as they evolve.

Nintendo is a prime example of a brand that leverages nostalgia. Generations of gamers grew up with Nintendo consoles and characters like Mario and Zelda. While the company has innovated with new technology, it never strays too far from its roots. Nintendo's ability to tap into childhood memories and nostalgia has kept the brand relevant, even as new gaming systems enter the market. The emotional connection to the past helps Nintendo maintain an iconic status in the gaming world.

Creating rituals

Another key to the psychology of iconic brands is the creation of rituals. Brands that embed themselves into the daily lives of their customers through rituals—whether it's a morning coffee routine or the experience of opening a new product—build lasting emotional connections.

Consider Nespresso. They've turned the act of making coffee into a ritualized experience. The tactile act of selecting a pod, hearing the machine hum, and watching the espresso pour out has become a part of their customers' daily routine. By transforming a simple task into a pleasurable ritual, Nespresso has created a strong emotional bond with their audience.

These rituals go beyond utility—they provide comfort, joy, and a sense of consistency in a world that's often chaotic.

The lasting impact of iconic brands

The psychology of iconic brands lies in their ability to connect deeply with people's emotions, identities, and values. They aren't just about the product—they're about what the product represents. By standing for something meaningful, offering self-expression, remaining consistent, staying culturally relevant, and tapping into nostalgia and rituals, these brands carve out a permanent place in the hearts and minds of their audience.

As we move forward, we'll explore how storytelling plays a crucial role in building these emotional connections. Next, we'll dive into *The storytelling power: Feel first, think later* and discover how stories can transform brands into unforgettable experiences.

Storytelling power: Feel first, think later

In branding, logic isn't what wins over your audience—emotion is. And the most powerful tool to evoke that emotion? Storytelling. Stories have a unique ability to bypass our logical defenses and tap directly into our emotions, making us feel before we even start to think. This is why storytelling is one of the most effective strategies for creating memorable and emotionally resonant brands.

Think about it: people may forget facts and figures, but they rarely forget a good story. The brands that understand this are the ones that stand out, not because of their product's technical superiority, but because they make people *feel* something.

Why stories matter

From ancient times to today, humans have used stories to make sense of the world. Stories engage our brains in ways that raw information can't. When we hear a compelling story, our minds connect the dots, visualize the scene, and relate emotionally to the characters and events. It's this deep emotional engagement that makes storytelling such a powerful branding tool.

Brands that tell great stories don't just sell products—they create experiences. They transport their audience into a world where the brand becomes part of the customer's personal journey. Stories make your brand relatable, memorable, and most importantly, human.

The emotional hook

Great stories start by connecting with the audience's emotions. Before the product or service enters the picture, the focus is on the emotional journey of the characters or the story's arc. This could be a story of overcoming challenges, achieving a dream, or discovering something new about oneself. When your brand taps into these universal emotional experiences, it becomes more than just a logo or a product—it becomes part of the story itself.

Think about how Airbnb tells its story. Rather than focusing on features like price or convenience, Airbnb leans into the emotional experience of travel—connecting with new people, discovering new places, and feeling like you belong anywhere in the world. The story is about the adventure of travel and the comfort of feeling at home, no matter where you are. It's this emotional hook that draws people in.

Relatability and authenticity

For a story to resonate, it needs to be relatable and authentic. People are tired of overly polished, corporate-sounding messages. They want something real—stories that reflect their own experiences, values, or aspirations. Brands that tell authentic stories build trust, because they feel human and imperfect, just like the people they serve.

Look at Burt's Bees, a brand that started with a simple story: two founders making homemade beeswax products on a small farm. They didn't try to be slick or polished—they embraced their down-to-earth, natural origins, which resonated with consumers who valued authenticity and environmental responsibility. Burt's Bees' success is rooted in their ability to tell an authentic story that aligns with their brand's values.

Storytelling through experience

Some of the best brand stories are told through experiences, not words. Think of a brand like Disney. Disney doesn't just tell stories through its movies—it creates entire worlds where the brand story comes to life. The experience of visiting a Disney theme park is an immersive journey where visitors become part of the story, whether they're walking through Cinderella's castle or flying with Peter Pan. Disney's storytelling power lies in making customers feel like they're part of the magic.

This principle can be applied across industries. Retail brands like Lush, for instance, turn shopping into a sensory experience. When you walk into a Lush store, you're hit with vibrant colors, natural scents, and interactive product demonstrations. It's not just about buying soap—it's about experiencing the brand's commitment to ethical, handmade products. By creating an immersive experience, Lush tells a story of sustainability, creativity, and care.

Building brand identity through narrative

Storytelling also plays a crucial role in shaping a brand's identity. When done well, a brand's story reinforces what the company stands for and why it matters. This narrative becomes the backbone of the brand's identity, guiding everything from marketing campaigns to product design.

Warby Parker is a great example of a brand that has built its identity around a strong narrative. The founders started the company after discovering how expensive eyewear was due to industry monopolies. They wanted to create affordable, stylish glasses while also giving back to those in need. Warby Parker's brand identity is rooted in this story of democratizing access to eyewear and helping communities around the world. This narrative isn't just a marketing tactic—it's a fundamental part of their brand DNA, which resonates deeply with their audience.

The hero's journey

One of the most effective storytelling structures is the hero's journey—a classic narrative arc where the hero faces challenges, overcomes obstacles, and emerges transformed. Many iconic brands use this structure to tell stories about their customers as heroes on their own journeys.

Nike's "Just Do It" campaign is built around this idea. The customer isn't just buying a pair of shoes—they're the hero of their own fitness journey. Nike's storytelling consistently highlights athletes, both professional and everyday people, overcoming adversity, pushing past their limits, and achieving greatness. Nike positions itself as the brand that helps you conquer your personal challenges, making the customer the hero.

Telling your brand's story

So, how can your brand harness the power of storytelling? Start by identifying your brand's core values and mission. What drives your company beyond profit? What change are you trying to create in the world? Once you have these answers, you can craft a story that resonates with your audience's emotions, values, and aspirations.

Focus on the people in your story—whether it's your customers, employees, or even the brand founders. Make the story relatable and personal. Your audience should see themselves in the narrative, whether they're solving a problem, discovering a passion, or connecting with a larger purpose.

Remember, it's not about making the product the hero—it's about making the customer the hero and showing how your brand is part of their journey.

Feel first, think later

When you focus on storytelling, you tap into a powerful truth: people feel first and think later. By leading with emotion and following up with logic, you create deeper, more meaningful connections with your audience. Storytelling turns your brand from a company into a trusted companion, one that your customers will choose time and time again because they believe in the story you're telling.

Next, we'll look at case studies that highlight how some of the most successful brands have used storytelling to create lasting loyalty. Join us as we explore how *Apple, Starbucks, and others* have harnessed the power of emotional storytelling.

Case studies: Apple, Starbucks, and loyalty

Loyalty is the holy grail for any brand. It's what keeps customers coming back, even when competitors offer similar products or better prices. But loyalty doesn't happen by chance. It's the result of creating an emotional connection that makes people feel attached to your brand. Apple and Starbucks are masters of building loyalty—not just through the quality of their products, but through the stories they tell, the communities they build, and the values they uphold.

Let's dive into how these brands use storytelling and emotional branding to cultivate fierce loyalty.

Apple: A brand built on identity

Apple's success goes beyond its sleek products and cutting-edge technology. What truly sets Apple apart is its ability to make people feel like they belong to something bigger. Apple is more than a company; it's a symbol of creativity, innovation, and individuality. From the very beginning, Apple's story has been about challenging the status quo and empowering people to "Think Different."

Apple's storytelling reinforces the idea that owning an Apple product makes you part of a community of forward-thinkers and trailblazers. This is why people line up for hours outside Apple stores for the latest iPhone. It's not just about the phone—it's about being part of a movement that values design, innovation, and breaking free from the ordinary.

By consistently reinforcing these values through their marketing, product design, and customer experience, Apple has created a loyal following that sees the brand as part of their identity. Apple customers don't just use the products—they believe in the brand's vision. This deep emotional connection is why Apple has such high customer retention and brand loyalty.

Starbucks: Selling more than coffee

Starbucks isn't just a place to grab a cup of coffee—it's a "third place" between home and work where people can relax, connect, and recharge. The brand has turned an everyday habit into an emotional experience, using storytelling and community-building to create a sense of belonging.

From the beginning, Starbucks focused on creating an inviting atmosphere where people could linger. Their stores are designed to be warm, comfortable spaces that encourage conversation and connection. This sense of community is a huge part of why Starbucks has such a loyal customer base. It's not just about the coffee; it's about the experience of being in a Starbucks, the smell of freshly brewed beans, the personal interaction with baristas, and the feeling of being part of a global community.

Starbucks has also been highly effective in personalizing the customer experience. With their rewards program and app, they've created a direct connection with their customers, offering tailored rewards and perks that keep people coming back. Every cup of coffee isn't just a transaction—it's part of an ongoing relationship.

The loyalty formula: Emotional connection + consistency

Both Apple and Starbucks use a similar formula for building loyalty: emotional connection plus consistency. They don't rely solely on the quality of their products (though that's a given); instead, they focus on creating an emotional experience that customers can count on.

With Apple, the emotional connection comes from the brand's identity and values. With Starbucks, it's about the experience of comfort, personalization, and community. But both brands are relentless in maintaining consistency across all touchpoints. Whether you're buying an iPhone in New York or Sydney, the experience is seamless. The same goes for Starbucks—no matter which location you visit, you know exactly what to expect.

Consistency builds trust, and trust leads to loyalty. When customers know they can rely on your brand for a consistent, positive experience, they're far more likely to stay loyal.

Building communities, not just customer bases

Another key to loyalty is creating a sense of belonging. Apple has mastered this by creating a community of users who feel like they're part of something special. Whether it's through their sleek, minimalist designs or their groundbreaking products, Apple makes its customers feel like they're part of a movement.

Starbucks has built a similar sense of community. The "third place" concept has created a space where people feel comfortable spending time, whether they're meeting friends, catching up on work, or just enjoying a moment of peace. Starbucks stores have become social hubs, and that sense of community fosters deep brand loyalty.

The role of values in building loyalty

Loyalty isn't just about emotional connection—it's also about shared values. Both Apple and Starbucks have built loyalty by aligning with the values of their customers.

For Apple, it's about innovation, creativity, and simplicity. The brand stands for pushing boundaries and thinking differently, and customers who share those values feel deeply connected to the brand. They don't just buy Apple products; they buy into Apple's mission of challenging the status quo.

Starbucks, on the other hand, has built loyalty through its commitment to sustainability, ethical sourcing, and community engagement. By promoting fair trade coffee, reducing waste, and supporting local communities, Starbucks connects with customers who care about these issues. This alignment of values strengthens the emotional bond between the brand and its customers, making loyalty much more than just a preference for a particular coffee brand.

Loyalty through personalization

Personalization plays a crucial role in building loyalty, and both Apple and Starbucks have leveraged this to deepen their relationships with customers. Apple personalizes the user experience with features like iCloud, iMessage, and the seamless integration across all Apple devices. This creates a personal, unified ecosystem where everything feels tailor-made for the user.

Starbucks has done this through their rewards app, where customers earn points for every purchase and receive personalized offers based on their preferences. This level of personalization makes customers feel valued, reinforcing their loyalty to the brand.

Lessons for your brand

So, what can your brand learn from Apple and Starbucks? Loyalty isn't just about delivering great products—it's about building emotional connections, creating consistent experiences, and aligning with your customers' values. When people feel emotionally connected to your brand, they're not just buying your product—they're buying into your story, your mission, and your community.

The next section will explore how iconic brands create unforgettable, lasting brand assets. We'll look at *The Coca-Cola effect* and why sensory branding plays a crucial role in building brand loyalty.

CHAPTER 05

CREATING BRAND ASSETS THAT STICK

The Coca-Cola effect: Sensory branding

Close your eyes for a moment and imagine the sound of a Coca-Cola can being popped open. The crisp fizz, the rush of carbonation—it's a sound many of us instantly recognize. Now, picture the unmistakable red can, the white script, and the swirling bottle shape. Maybe you can even recall the refreshing taste or the cold condensation on your hand. This is the power of sensory branding: a brand experience that doesn't just reach the mind—it engages the senses.

Coca-Cola has mastered sensory branding, creating associations so powerful that just a glimpse or a sound can trigger memories and emotions. This is the essence of *The Coca-Cola effect*—when a brand goes beyond logos and slogans and becomes a multi-sensory experience that is nearly impossible to forget.

The five senses: A gateway to emotion

We experience the world through our five senses—sight, sound, touch, taste, and smell. Brands that engage multiple senses have a stronger chance of creating lasting impressions. When your brand can tap into these senses, you're no longer just selling a product—you're creating an emotional experience that becomes part of your customers' lives.

Coca-Cola has done this brilliantly. Their iconic red and white colors are instantly recognizable, while the shape of the bottle is so distinct that people can identify it even when it's smashed. The crisp sound of opening a Coke and the familiar, sweet taste all work together to create a sensory experience that sticks with people long after the product is consumed.

But Coca-Cola's success isn't just about the individual senses—it's about how they all come together to create an experience that feels familiar, comforting, and enjoyable.

Visual identity: Making an instant impression

Of all the senses, sight is perhaps the most immediately impactful. A strong visual identity can grab attention and create a connection before a single word is spoken. Coca-Cola's use of its distinct red color, bold white script, and instantly recognizable bottle has become a blueprint for iconic visual branding. Their visual identity hasn't just been consistent—it's become part of the cultural fabric.

But it's not just Coca-Cola. Think of Tiffany & Co. The brand's signature robin's egg blue box is synonymous with luxury, elegance, and special moments. Tiffany's doesn't need to plaster its logo all over its packaging—the color alone evokes feelings of sophistication and excitement.

For brands looking to replicate this effect, the key is consistency and distinctiveness. Colors, shapes, and designs should not only be recognizable but also evoke the emotions and experiences you want your customers to associate with your brand.

Sound branding: The emotional trigger

Sound has a unique way of triggering emotions and memories. Just a few notes can evoke nostalgia, excitement, or a sense of calm. Coca-Cola has incorporated sound into its branding through the simple act of opening a can or bottle. The fizzing carbonation is a sensory cue that many people associate with refreshment and satisfaction.

Sound branding goes beyond jingles and music. Intel's signature five-note chime, for example, has become synonymous with technology and innovation. Netflix's "ta-dum" sound before every show or movie creates an association with entertainment and relaxation. These sound cues are short, simple, but incredibly effective at embedding a brand into people's minds.

The power of sound branding lies in its ability to be subtle but impactful. It doesn't need to shout—it simply needs to be consistent and aligned with your brand's identity.

Taste and smell: Deep sensory connection

For food and beverage brands, taste and smell are powerful tools for building brand loyalty. Coca-Cola's taste is proprietary and unmistakable. People often say they can taste the difference between Coke and its competitors—and whether that's psychological or real, it's a testament to how strong the brand's taste identity is.

Smell is closely linked to memory and emotion. Think about walking into a bakery and the smell of fresh bread triggering memories of childhood. Brands like Cinnabon capitalize on this by ensuring their stores are filled with the aroma of cinnamon rolls, enticing people to come in and experience the product. Smell has the unique ability to transport people emotionally, and when a brand can create a signature scent, it becomes part of the overall sensory experience.

While not every brand can leverage taste and smell, for those in industries like food, beverages, or even beauty and retail, these senses are invaluable tools for creating deeper emotional connections.

Touch: The often-overlooked sense

Touch is another crucial element of sensory branding, even though it's often overlooked. The feel of a product—whether it's the sleek design of a smartphone, the softness of a luxury blanket, or the weight of a high-end watch—adds to the overall perception of quality and experience.

Coca-Cola even considers the tactile experience of holding a bottle. The glass contour bottle, for instance, was designed to feel just right in your hand, creating an emotional connection beyond the drink itself. When a product feels premium or unique in your hand, it can elevate the overall brand experience.

Brands like Apple have also mastered touch. The unboxing experience of an Apple product is tactile and deliberate. From the smooth finish of their packaging to the way their devices fit perfectly in hand, Apple has turned touch into a key part of their brand experience.

Creating your sensory brand

So how do you build a sensory brand? It's about crafting an experience that engages multiple senses in a consistent and meaningful way. Start by thinking about what sensory elements make sense for your brand. Is there a color that can become synonymous with your identity? A sound that can evoke a feeling? A texture that enhances your product's quality?

The goal is to create a brand experience that becomes embedded in your customers' lives. Sensory branding isn't just about the product—it's about how the product makes people feel, and how that feeling creates loyalty.

The Coca-Cola effect in action

The Coca-Cola effect shows us the power of sensory branding. By creating a multi-sensory experience that engages sight, sound, taste, touch, and even smell, Coca-Cola has turned a simple drink into a cultural icon. It's not just the product—it's the way the product is experienced.

Your brand might not be selling beverages, but the lesson is universal. Engage the senses, and you engage your customers on a deeper, more emotional level. When people can see, hear, feel, or even taste your brand, it becomes much harder to forget.

Next, we'll explore *Why recall matters* and how building sticky, memorable brand elements helps you stay top of mind in a world full of distractions.

Why recall matters

Today consumers are bombarded with information and choices, staying top of mind is no small feat. Brands that succeed are the ones people can recall quickly and easily when they're ready to make a purchase. This ability to be remembered, or "brand recall," is critical to building loyalty, driving sales, and ensuring long-term success.

When consumers are faced with endless options, they'll choose the brand they remember most. If your brand is forgettable, it doesn't matter how great your product or service is—someone else will capture the sale. That's why brand recall is so important. It's not just about recognition; it's about being the *first* brand that comes to mind when your customer has a need.

The psychology of brand recall

Brand recall is all about mental availability. It's about making sure your brand occupies a key place in the customer's memory, so when a relevant need arises, they think of you first. The brain organizes information through repetition and emotional connections. The more frequently someone sees, hears, or experiences your brand in meaningful ways, the more likely they are to recall it.

Think about everyday decisions—choosing a place to grab coffee, a brand of sneakers, or a type of toothpaste. The brands that come to mind first often win the sale, not necessarily because they're the best product, but because they've built strong mental availability. Brands like Nike, Starbucks, and Colgate have created such strong recall that, in their respective categories, they're often synonymous with the product itself.

The first-to-mind advantage

The brand that comes to mind first has a distinct advantage. In many cases, consumers won't even consider other options if a brand already feels like a familiar choice. This is why being top-of-mind matters so much. If your brand is the first to come up in a consumer's mental "search engine," you're more likely to get the sale without your customer shopping around.

This is where consistency in branding plays a crucial role. The more consistently you present your brand across different touchpoints—advertising, packaging, social media, customer service—the stronger your recall will be. Repetition isn't just about frequency; it's about consistent messaging that reinforces your brand's identity and promise.

How to build brand recall

So, how do you ensure your brand is remembered? It starts with creating *sticky* brand elements that leave a lasting impression. Here are a few ways to build strong brand recall:

1. **Distinctive assets**: Your logo, colors, typography, and design elements should be instantly recognizable. Think about McDonald's golden arches or Nike's swoosh—these are simple but highly memorable visual cues that make recall almost automatic. The simpler and more distinct your assets, the easier they are to remember.

2. **Consistent messaging**: Your brand's message should be clear, consistent, and repeated across all channels. Whether it's in your advertising, website copy, or social media posts, your message needs to reinforce who you are and why you matter. The more consistent your message, the more familiar your brand feels, which leads to stronger recall.

3. **Emotional connections**: Brands that evoke emotions are far more likely to be remembered. When people feel something—whether it's excitement, nostalgia, or trust—they're more likely to store that experience in their memory. Coca-Cola's "Share a Coke" campaign wasn't just about the product; it was about the emotional experience of sharing something meaningful with someone else. That emotional connection boosts recall.

4. **Storytelling**: Stories are inherently memorable. They help people organize information in a way that sticks. Brands that tell compelling stories about who they are and what they stand for create deeper emotional and psychological connections. Apple doesn't just sell technology—they tell stories about innovation, creativity, and challenging the status quo. Those stories make the brand memorable long after the product has been purchased.

5. **Repetition and frequency**: It may sound basic, but repetition is key. The more often someone sees or interacts with your brand, the stronger the recall will be. This doesn't mean bombarding your audience with ads, but it does mean being present where your audience is—whether that's through social media, email marketing, or other touchpoints.

When brand recall drives loyalty

Strong brand recall leads to more than just a one-time sale—it builds long-term loyalty. When customers can recall your brand effortlessly, they're more likely to develop a sense of trust and familiarity. Over time, this leads to repeat purchases and deepens customer loyalty.

Loyalty is often a byproduct of brand familiarity. Customers are more comfortable buying from a brand they know and recognize than taking a risk on something unfamiliar. That's why brands like Amazon, which have become deeply ingrained in consumers' lives, enjoy such high levels of loyalty. People don't just recall Amazon when they need something—they default to it, because it's familiar, trusted, and reliable.

Staying top of mind in a noisy world

The challenge for brands today is staying top of mind in a world full of distractions. Consumers are exposed to thousands of brands, messages, and ads every day. Cutting through that noise requires a mix of creativity, consistency, and strategic positioning.

Brands that stay top of mind do more than just advertise—they create experiences. They offer value through content, community, and engagement that goes beyond the traditional sales pitch. Patagonia, for example, stays top of mind by actively promoting its environmental mission and sharing stories of conservation and sustainability. The brand isn't just selling products; it's building a movement that people want to be part of.

Recall in the digital age

The rise of digital and social media has changed how brands approach recall. In the past, brands relied heavily on traditional advertising to maintain awareness. Today, social media, influencer marketing, and even customer reviews play a crucial role in keeping a brand top of mind.

One of the most effective ways to build recall digitally is through content marketing. By creating valuable, shareable content—whether it's blog posts, videos, or social media updates—your brand stays visible and relevant. This ongoing engagement helps keep your brand in the consumer's mental rotation, ready to be recalled when the need arises.

The long game

Building brand recall isn't a short-term play—it's a long game. It requires consistency, strategic touchpoints, and a commitment to reinforcing your brand message over time. But the payoff is worth it. When your brand becomes the first thing people think of in your category, you're no longer just competing—you're leading.

The next section will explore *Building sticky brand elements*—the visual, auditory, and experiential cues that help ensure your brand stays lodged in the minds of your audience.

Building sticky brand elements

What makes a brand unforgettable? It's not just a clever logo or a catchy slogan—truly sticky brand elements are the ones that leave a lasting impression on the consumer's mind. These elements are so distinctive and memorable that they instantly evoke the brand, even in a crowded marketplace.

Sticky brand elements go beyond visual identity. They include sensory cues, experiences, and emotions that make a brand stand out. When done right, these elements become deeply embedded in the consumer's mind, making your brand the first one they think of when they need your product or service.

The power of simplicity

One of the hallmarks of sticky brand elements is simplicity. The most memorable brands aren't overcomplicated—they use clear, simple visuals and messages that are easy to recognize and recall. Think about Nike's swoosh or McDonald's golden arches. These symbols are not only iconic, but they're also incredibly simple. There's no clutter, no confusion—just clean, recognizable imagery that sticks in your memory.

When crafting your brand elements, focus on clarity and simplicity. Your logo, typography, and colors should be distinct, but not overwhelming. The easier it is for people to recognize your brand at a glance, the more likely they are to remember it.

Consistency breeds familiarity

Consistency is key when building sticky brand elements. Your customers need to see the same logo, colors, and messaging across all touchpoints—whether it's on your website, social media, packaging, or in-store. When you show up the same way, again and again, it builds familiarity. And familiarity leads to trust.

Look at Coca-Cola. Their use of the iconic red and white color scheme and the flowing script logo has been consistent for decades. Even if you only catch a glimpse of the color red and the signature font, you immediately think of Coke. That level of brand recall comes from years of consistent visual presentation. When your brand elements are consistent, they become more powerful over time.

Emotionally charged elements

The most powerful brand elements aren't just visual—they evoke emotion. A logo or sound that triggers an emotional response creates a deeper connection with your audience, making your brand not just recognizable but meaningful.

Consider the jingle for Intel's "Intel Inside" campaign. Those five musical notes are simple, but they create an emotional response tied to innovation and reliability. The emotional charge behind a sound or image makes it much more memorable. Whether it's a jingle, a brand scent, or a tagline, your goal should be to evoke a feeling that goes beyond the rational and taps into the emotional.

Visual identity: More than just a logo

Your logo is a critical part of your brand's visual identity, but it's not the only thing that matters. Every visual element—from your color palette to your packaging design—plays a role in how memorable your brand is. When these visual cues are cohesive and well thought out, they reinforce each other, making the entire brand experience more impactful.

Take Tiffany & Co., for example. The brand's iconic robin's egg blue is as much a part of its identity as the jewelry itself. The color has become synonymous with luxury and elegance. It's so powerful that even without the logo, people instantly recognize the brand by the color alone. When every visual element is aligned, it creates a brand experience that's hard to forget.

The role of sound and scent

Brands that engage the senses create a more immersive and memorable experience. Sound, in particular, can be a powerful tool for building brand recall. Audio branding—whether it's a jingle, a signature sound, or a tone—creates an instant connection with your brand. Think of Netflix's "ta-dum" sound. It's only two notes, but it's so closely tied to the Netflix experience that hearing it instantly evokes thoughts of binge-watching your favorite shows.

Scent can also be a powerful brand element. Some hotels use signature scents in their lobbies, creating an immediate emotional connection with guests. The scent becomes part of the brand's identity, creating a sense of comfort and familiarity. When customers smell that scent again, they're reminded of the brand experience, even when they're not in the hotel.

Building rituals around your brand

Sticky brand elements aren't just about what people see or hear—they're also about the experiences you create. Brands that build rituals around their products or services make themselves unforgettable. A ritualized experience becomes a key part of the customer's routine, making the brand essential to their daily lives.

Consider Nespresso, a brand that has turned the act of making coffee into a ritual. From choosing the perfect pod to the sound of the machine brewing, Nespresso creates an experience that is more than just about drinking coffee. This ritual creates a deep connection with the brand, making it hard for customers to switch to competitors.

The impact of nostalgia

Nostalgia is another powerful tool for building sticky brand elements. When brands evoke positive memories from the past, they create emotional bonds that are hard to break. Whether it's through a throwback logo, a vintage product design, or a campaign that taps into childhood memories, nostalgia can make a brand feel familiar and comforting.

Nintendo has leveraged nostalgia to great effect. The brand consistently reintroduces classic games and characters, tapping into the memories of gamers who grew up playing Nintendo in their youth. This connection to the past strengthens the bond between the brand and its audience, keeping it relevant across generations.

Staying relevant while being consistent

While consistency is key, brands also need to evolve. A brand that becomes too rigid risks feeling outdated or irrelevant. The challenge is to maintain consistency while adapting to changing trends and customer expectations.

Brands like Lego have mastered this balance. While the brand's core visual elements have stayed the same—bright colors, interlocking bricks—Lego has evolved its product line to stay relevant in a digital age. By introducing new themes, partnerships, and even video games, Lego keeps its brand elements consistent while staying fresh.

Making your brand unforgettable

Sticky brand elements are about more than just being recognizable—they're about creating experiences that leave a lasting impression. Whether it's through a signature color, a memorable sound, or a ritualized product experience, the brands that stay with us are the ones that engage multiple senses and evoke strong emotions.

When your brand elements are simple, consistent, and emotionally charged, they become part of your audience's everyday lives. And when that happens, your brand is no longer just a choice—it's a habit.

Next, we'll dive into some case studies that show how brands like McDonald's and Netflix have built some of the stickiest brand elements in the world—and why they continue to lead in recall and loyalty.

Case studies: McDonald's and Netflix

Some brands don't just create sticky brand elements—they redefine how brand elements can shape consumer behavior and loyalty.

McDonald's and Netflix have both mastered the art of embedding their brand deeply into everyday life, building experiences that stick with people long after the initial interaction.

Let's take a closer look at how these two powerhouse brands have built brand elements that are instantly recognizable, consistently engaging, and impossible to forget.

McDonald's: The power of sensory branding

McDonald's has become one of the most recognizable brands in the world, largely due to its mastery of sensory branding. From its iconic golden arches to the jingle that everyone can hum—"I'm Lovin' It"—McDonald's has created a multi-sensory experience that goes far beyond fast food.

The golden arches: A symbol of consistency

The golden arches are among the most recognizable logos globally. They aren't just a logo—they are a symbol of consistency. Whether you're in New York, Tokyo, or Johannesburg, seeing those arches triggers a sense of familiarity. You know exactly what you'll get when you walk in—a consistent experience, reliable food, and an atmosphere that feels the same no matter where you are.

This visual identity is a key part of why McDonald's has become so sticky. It's not just about the food; it's about the feeling of predictability and comfort the brand provides. The golden arches have transcended fast food, becoming a symbol of childhood nostalgia, family outings, and convenience.

The jingle that sticks

Music and sound are powerful tools for embedding a brand into people's minds, and McDonald's has used this to great effect with their "I'm Lovin' It" jingle. Even if you haven't been to a McDonald's in years, you can probably recall the tune instantly. This simple, catchy jingle is a classic example of how sound branding can create long-lasting recall.

By pairing the visual power of the golden arches with the audio cue of the jingle, McDonald's has built a brand that stays with people on multiple sensory levels. These elements create an emotional connection that goes beyond the food, making McDonald's more than just a restaurant—it's a brand experience.

A sensory experience

It's not just the visual and audio elements that make McDonald's sticky. The brand also engages other senses, like smell and taste. The smell of McDonald's fries is distinctive, and for many, it brings back memories of family road trips or quick stops after a busy day. This sensory experience, combined with the brand's other elements, creates a multi-layered emotional connection.

McDonald's has mastered how to make its brand elements work together to create a consistent and recognizable experience that sticks with people worldwide.

Netflix: Mastering recall through experience

Netflix has taken a completely different approach to building sticky brand elements, focusing primarily on the experience of entertainment. The brand has managed to become synonymous with relaxation, binge-watching, and entertainment itself. Netflix's approach to brand building isn't centered on visual elements, but rather on how its service fits into people's everyday lives.

The "ta-dum" sound

Netflix's signature two-note "ta-dum" sound is simple, but incredibly powerful. Every time you hear it, you know exactly what's coming—hours of entertainment, whether it's your favorite show or a new movie. This sound has become Netflix's auditory signature, an instant cue that triggers excitement and anticipation for viewers.

Much like McDonald's jingle, Netflix's "ta-dum" sound has become an emotional trigger for people. It's associated with relaxation, enjoyment, and the simple pleasure of kicking back to watch something entertaining. This use of sound branding builds recall in a subtle but powerful way, reinforcing the Netflix brand every time the service is used.

The ritual of binge-watching

Netflix has done more than just build sound and visual brand elements—it has created a new kind of consumer ritual. Binge-watching, once seen as a guilty pleasure, has become a normalized behavior, thanks to Netflix's model of releasing entire seasons at once. The act of sitting down to watch multiple episodes in a row has become synonymous with the Netflix brand.

This ritual is incredibly sticky. It creates a habitual behavior around the brand, making Netflix a go-to for entertainment. Over time, this repeated behavior strengthens brand loyalty and recall—people associate Netflix not just with content, but with the experience of binge-watching itself.

Personalized experiences

Netflix has also built brand loyalty through personalized experiences. The platform's algorithm tailors recommendations based on user preferences, making the service feel unique to each individual. This personalization not only enhances the user experience but also strengthens brand recall. When people think of Netflix, they don't just think of a generic streaming service—they think of "their" Netflix, tailored to their tastes and preferences.

This combination of personalized experiences and ritualized behavior creates a deep emotional connection between the brand and its users. Netflix has built an experience that is hard to walk away from because it feels so personal and integral to everyday entertainment.

Lessons from McDonald's and Netflix

What makes McDonald's and Netflix so effective at creating sticky brand elements is their ability to engage multiple senses and build rituals around their brand experiences. Whether it's through consistent visual identity, memorable sound cues, or creating new consumer behaviors, both brands have embedded themselves deeply into everyday life.

The key takeaway? Building sticky brand elements isn't just about logos and slogans—it's about creating experiences that people can feel, hear, and even smell. When you engage multiple senses and create rituals around your brand, you become more than just a product or service—you become a part of your customer's daily routine.

Next, we'll explore how your brand can carve out a unique space in the marketplace and how *Positioning your brand* helps define your place in a crowded world of competitors.

CHAPTER 06

POSITIONING YOUR BRAND

Carving out your unique space

Every brand has the potential to stand alone in its own niche. However, it's not enough to just stand out—you have to stand for something that resonates deeply with your audience. The key is not simply being different for the sake of it, but finding a way to define yourself that is meaningful, memorable, and valuable to the customers you serve.

The question isn't "How can I get noticed?" but rather "How can I create a position that's impossible to ignore?"

Focus on what truly sets you apart

Understanding what truly makes your brand distinctive is the foundation for creating a space that's yours and yours alone. Some brands focus on product quality, others on innovation, and many find their strength in a set of core values or purpose that connects with their audience.

Take REI, for example. They are much more than a seller of outdoor equipment. By centering their brand on environmental stewardship and outdoor adventure, they've created a narrative that resonates deeply with those who are passionate about nature. This focus is clear not just in their products but in the way they communicate and engage with their community.

Your differentiation should be rooted in authenticity—something real that no one else can claim.

Solving unmet needs

Finding an unaddressed problem or a gap in the market gives you a powerful way to position yourself. Customers often have needs or frustrations that competitors aren't addressing. If your brand can fill that void, it creates a lasting connection with your audience.

Dollar Shave Club is a great example of a brand that built its unique space by solving a practical problem: overpriced razors and the inconvenience of buying them. Their subscription model wasn't just convenient; it was an opportunity to challenge the norms of the shaving industry. By providing a straightforward solution, Dollar Shave Club carved out a loyal customer base in a saturated market.

Clarity and focus over trying to be everything

Brands that try to appeal to everyone often lose their way. Specialization, rather than generalization, can be the secret to finding and owning your space. Brands that focus on a specific niche or unique value proposition often find more loyal and passionate customers because they're offering something that feels tailor-made for them.

Warby Parker, for instance, didn't aim to be the go-to store for every type of eyewear. Instead, they specialized in affordable, stylish glasses with a direct-to-consumer model that was simple and accessible. Their focus allowed them to stand out in a traditionally expensive market, and their story of making eyewear accessible helped them connect on a deeper level with customers.

Owning your narrative

Your story is one of the most powerful tools you have to define your space. Customers don't just buy products—they buy into the brand's narrative and values. A compelling story makes your brand relatable, human, and memorable.

Patagonia, for instance, has built its brand on the narrative of environmental activism. They aren't just selling outdoor gear—they're encouraging their customers to be more thoughtful about consumption and their impact on the planet. Patagonia's purpose-driven story is what differentiates them from countless other outdoor brands, and that story resonates deeply with their audience.

The goal is to tell a story that feels authentic, aligns with your audience's values, and gives them a reason to choose you over competitors.

Finding untapped opportunities

Sometimes, the best way to carve out your space is to create it from scratch. Tesla didn't just enter the car market—they redefined what consumers could expect from a car company. By going all-in on electric vehicles and sustainable energy, Tesla tapped into a space that wasn't fully explored by competitors. They didn't just differentiate—they created a new category that they continue to dominate.

To find your brand's own white space, look at where others are falling short or where there's room to innovate. By being the first or the best at something no one else is doing, you create a distinct identity that's hard to replicate.

Staying consistent to maintain your position

Once you've found your space, consistency is critical. Brands that shift their focus too often risk losing the very differentiation they've worked so hard to build. Staying true to your core values and offering is key to maintaining trust and loyalty.

Lego has mastered this balance. While constantly evolving with new themes and partnerships, they have never strayed from their central identity of creativity and fun. This consistency has allowed them to stay relevant while maintaining the foundation of what makes them unique.

Positioning vs. differentiation

In branding, positioning and differentiation are often used interchangeably, but they serve distinct purposes. Both are essential to building a successful brand, yet they operate in different spaces within a brand's strategy. To truly stand out, you need to master both.

Differentiation is about what makes your brand unique—it's how you're different from your competitors. Positioning, on the other hand, is about where you stand in the mind of the customer. It's not just about being different; it's about being *relevant* and creating a clear, favorable place for your brand in the market.

To carve out your unique space, you need both. Differentiation is the groundwork—it's what sets you apart—but positioning is what ensures that your uniqueness is perceived as valuable by your audience.

Differentiation: Standing out in a sea of sameness

Differentiation is the process of defining what makes your brand distinct. What do you do better than your competitors? What value do you offer that no one else can claim? This is where your unique selling proposition (USP) comes into play.

When it comes to differentiation, you want to focus on what's truly meaningful to your audience. Gimmicks or surface-level differences won't sustain a brand over time. Instead, your differentiation should be built on something that resonates deeply with your customers, whether it's superior quality, innovation, or a set of shared values.

For example, Peloton isn't just another fitness brand. Their differentiation lies in the community they've built through their interactive classes and live streaming workouts. It's not just about the equipment—they offer an experience that allows users to connect, compete, and stay motivated. This distinction has helped Peloton rise above countless other fitness brands.

Positioning: Where you live in the customer's mind

Positioning is how your brand is perceived in the minds of your customers. It's not just about being different; it's about making sure that difference matters to the people you want to reach. Successful positioning occurs when your brand's uniqueness aligns with your audience's needs, desires, or values.

Apple —again— has mastered the art of positioning. The brand isn't positioned as just another tech company—it's associated with creativity, innovation, and simplicity. While there are many tech brands with unique offerings, Apple's positioning is what keeps it front of mind for millions of consumers. By focusing on creativity and design, Apple has secured a lasting position that resonates with their audience, which is why customers pay premium prices for their products.

In contrast, Samsung, another tech giant, differentiates itself through innovation and cutting-edge technology. But their positioning is less about creativity and more about functionality and technological advancement. Both brands are highly differentiated, but their positioning places them in different mental spaces in the minds of consumers.

The interplay between positioning and differentiation

While differentiation is essential for standing out, positioning determines whether your uniqueness will matter. You can be different, but if that difference doesn't align with what your audience values, your brand may fail to gain traction. Positioning ensures that the differences you promote are perceived as beneficial, relevant, and worth paying attention to.

Tesla is another great example of how positioning and differentiation work together. Tesla's differentiation lies in its electric vehicle technology and commitment to sustainability. But what makes them stand out even more is their positioning. Tesla isn't just seen as an electric car company—it's positioned as a pioneer of the future of transportation. They've created a perception that they are leading the charge in a movement toward a cleaner, smarter world. Tesla's position appeals to both eco-conscious consumers and tech enthusiasts, ensuring that their differentiation resonates with a broad audience.

Why both matter for long-term success

Brands that differentiate without positioning often struggle to build loyalty. They might attract initial attention with their uniqueness, but without clear positioning, customers won't understand why that difference matters to them.

Conversely, brands that position themselves well without true differentiation risk being forgotten. Even with great messaging and a clear value proposition, if your brand doesn't offer something unique, it's easy to get lost in the crowd.

For long-term success, brands need to master both. Differentiation ensures you stand out, while positioning ensures that your audience understands and values your uniqueness.

Finding the sweet spot

To find the sweet spot between differentiation and positioning, start by answering two questions:

1. **What makes my brand unique?** This is your differentiation—the core elements that set you apart from the competition.

2. **How does my brand align with what my customers value?** This is your positioning—how you create relevance and meaning in the minds of your audience.

The key is to ensure that what makes you different is also what makes you valuable to your audience. When these two aspects align, you create a brand that's not only unique but also trusted, respected, and remembered.

Creating a lasting brand impression

Brands that succeed in both differentiation and positioning create lasting impressions. Their uniqueness is clear, and their message is relevant to the people they want to reach. More importantly, they've secured a place in their customer's mind that keeps them top of mind when a need arises.

Think of how Nike's differentiation (performance-driven, athlete-focused gear) works in harmony with its positioning (empowering athletes of all levels to achieve their potential). Their famous tagline, "Just Do It," is more than a slogan—it's a clear positioning statement that connects with anyone looking to push their limits. This powerful combination of differentiation and positioning has made Nike one of the most recognizable and successful brands in the world.

Next, we'll dive into the importance of storytelling in positioning your brand effectively and how crafting a compelling narrative can solidify your brand's place in the minds and hearts of your audience.

The importance of storytelling

Facts tell, but stories sell. In branding, storytelling is the secret weapon that transforms cold, hard data into compelling narratives that resonate on an emotional level. It's what turns a product into a movement, a service into a solution, and a brand into something deeply personal. Without a story, even the most differentiated brand can struggle to connect.

Great brands understand this: they don't just sell products—they tell stories that speak to their audience's aspirations, values, and emotions. Storytelling gives a brand meaning beyond its functionality, forging a connection that goes far deeper than a simple transaction.

Why stories work

Storytelling taps directly into the emotional part of the brain. While logic can inform, it's emotions that drive decisions. Stories have the unique ability to engage us, evoke feelings, and create a sense of connection. They make the abstract tangible and give us a reason to care.

Brands that excel at storytelling focus not just on what they do but why they do it, making their mission and purpose relatable. This humanizes the brand, turning it from a business into a trusted entity.

Take Lush, for example. The cosmetics brand's story isn't just about handmade beauty products—it's about ethical sourcing, environmental responsibility, and a commitment to animal welfare. This story elevates their brand beyond just the products they sell.

Consumers feel like they're supporting a greater cause when they buy from Lush, creating a bond that goes beyond mere shopping.

Making your audience the hero

The most effective brand stories aren't centered on the company—they make the customer the hero. When a brand shifts the focus to the audience, it creates a narrative that customers can see themselves in. This invites them to be part of the story.

A great example is GoPro. Rather than focusing on the technical specs of their cameras, GoPro showcases the extraordinary experiences their customers capture. The brand tells the stories of adventurers, athletes, and creators, using customer-generated content to highlight how the product enables them to live boldly. In this narrative, GoPro users are the heroes, with the camera playing a supporting role in capturing their best moments. It's this approach that has turned GoPro into a lifestyle brand, not just a camera company.

Building trust through authenticity

One of the key benefits of storytelling is its ability to build trust. When a brand shares an authentic story—whether it's about its origins, mission, or the people behind it—it becomes more relatable. Authenticity is the bedrock of trust, and consumers today are quick to connect with brands that feel genuine.

For instance, Burt's Bees built its brand story around authenticity and simplicity, starting with its founders making beeswax candles in a rural setting. The brand's continued focus on natural ingredients and environmental sustainability gives their story credibility and helps maintain a loyal customer base. Burt's Bees isn't just selling lip balm or skincare products—they're selling a back-to-basics, eco-friendly ethos that resonates deeply with their audience.

Stories create emotional connections

At its core, storytelling is about building emotional connections. When brands tell stories that align with their audience's values, they go from being a choice to being *the* choice. Emotional connections aren't built on product features—they're built on shared values, experiences, and aspirations.

Consider LEGO. The brand has been telling stories through its products for decades, helping children (and adults) use their imaginations to build worlds and create their own adventures. LEGO's storytelling isn't confined to advertisements—it's embedded in the very nature of its product, allowing customers to become the storytellers themselves. This narrative of creativity and limitless possibility strengthens LEGO's connection with its audience, keeping the brand relevant across generations.

Storytelling is not just a tool for marketing—it's the foundation of how your brand communicates with the world. A great story builds trust, fosters emotional connections, and makes your brand memorable. Whether it's by empowering customers to be part of the narrative or by staying true to your brand's mission, storytelling has the power to transform a brand from ordinary to unforgettable.

Next, we'll dive into how *Positioning your brand* helps carve out a clear and compelling space in the marketplace, ensuring your story reaches the right audience.

Mapping your brand's position

Where does your brand live in the mind of your customer? That's the question at the heart of brand positioning. It's not just about being different—it's about being the right kind of different for the audience you want to attract. Mapping your brand's position is the process of determining how your brand is perceived in comparison to your competitors and making sure that perception aligns with your values, your offerings, and the needs of your customers.

Positioning is about clarity. It's about ensuring that when your audience thinks of a particular need, your brand comes to mind as the best solution. But to achieve this, you first need to know where you currently stand and where you want to go.

The positioning map: Plotting the competitive landscape

A positioning map is a simple but powerful tool that helps visualize where your brand sits in the competitive landscape. By plotting different brands on a chart according to key attributes—such as price, quality, innovation, or customer experience—you can see how your brand compares and where potential opportunities for differentiation lie.

Imagine you're a brand in the smartphone industry. You might map your position based on factors like performance and design. Brands like Samsung or Google might sit on one end of the spectrum for advanced technology, while another brand may focus more on affordability and simplicity. If your brand is trying to offer cutting-edge innovation at a lower price point, you can easily spot gaps where your message can hit home and where competitors might be falling short.

Identifying your differentiators

Mapping your brand's position begins with identifying what truly sets you apart. What key attributes define your brand? These could be anything from exceptional customer service to innovative design or ethical sourcing. Once you understand these differentiators, you can map out how your strengths align with your competitors' weaknesses—or where there's an unclaimed space in the market.

Take Oatly, the oat milk brand that's carved out a distinct position in the dairy alternative market. While competitors focused on taste or price, Oatly leaned heavily into sustainability, environmental awareness, and their quirky, irreverent tone. Their differentiation isn't just in the product—it's in their purpose and how they communicate it. Oatly mapped a position that allowed them to become the voice of the climate-conscious consumer, setting themselves apart in a crowded space.

Understanding customer perception

Once you've identified your differentiators, it's important to check how your customers actually perceive your brand. Are they seeing you the way you want to be seen? This is where market research comes in—whether through surveys, focus groups, or data analysis, understanding customer perceptions is crucial to adjusting your positioning effectively.

For example, if you aim to position your brand as premium but customers see it as mid-tier, there's a disconnect. Closing that gap involves aligning your messaging, branding, and overall experience with the positioning you want to claim.

Mapping your position also helps you understand what your customers prioritize. If you discover that they care more about ethical production than cutting-edge innovation, you can adjust your positioning to reflect those values and stand out in a way that truly matters to your audience.

Flexibility in positioning

Your brand's position isn't static. It needs to evolve as your market shifts, as customer preferences change, and as new competitors emerge. What worked a decade ago might not hold up today. Look at how brands like Netflix have adapted—what began as a DVD rental service has morphed into a global entertainment platform. Netflix's original positioning was all about convenience, but they shifted their strategy over time to become synonymous with content creation and binge-worthy shows, keeping pace with customer expectations.

Staying relevant means being willing to adapt your position when necessary, while staying true to your core brand values. Mapping your brand's position regularly helps ensure that you're moving in sync with your audience.

Your map is your guide—but it's always a good idea to check in with your audience to see how the terrain is shifting.

Next, we'll dive into real-world case studies of how brands like Airbnb, Uber, and others have navigated their brand positioning to stand out in crowded markets.

Case studies: Uber, Dollar Shave Club

Some brands don't just position themselves in the marketplace—they disrupt it entirely. By carving out unique spaces, Uber and Dollar Shave Club didn't simply compete with their rivals; they redefined their industries. Their success stories are not just about innovation in services but also about how they positioned themselves as the solution to problems customers didn't even know they had.

Let's explore how these brands leveraged smart positioning to become game changers.

Uber: Reinventing transportation

Before Uber, the taxi industry was seen as inconvenient, outdated, and inconsistent. People were used to flagging down cabs, dealing with cash payments, and accepting unpredictable service quality. Uber's entry into the market didn't just introduce a new ride-sharing service—it changed how people thought about transportation entirely.

Uber positioned itself as more than just an alternative to taxis. It offered a faster, more convenient way to get around. The ability to hail a ride via an app, track your driver, and make cashless payments were revolutionary at the time. Uber framed itself as a tech company rather than a transportation service, highlighting its use of technology to provide real-time solutions. This differentiation from traditional taxi services allowed Uber to target tech-savvy urban professionals who were frustrated with the status quo.

Uber's marketing message wasn't about ridesharing alone—it was about empowering people with the freedom to move. Uber positioned itself as a service that's not only easy and reliable but one that gives control back to the rider. This framing helped the company stand out not just against taxis but against any form of traditional transportation. Over time, Uber's positioning evolved to include UberX, Uber Eats, and more, adapting to new markets while maintaining its identity as a technology-driven enabler of convenience.

Dollar Shave Club: Disrupting an entrenched industry

The razor industry was dominated by a few giants who dictated both the prices and the narrative. Buying razors meant dealing with overpriced products locked behind glass cabinets in drugstores, with customers often wondering why something so simple could cost so much. Dollar Shave Club stepped into this space with a bold, clear message: why pay more when you don't have to?

Dollar Shave Club's differentiation was obvious from the start—razors delivered directly to your door for a fraction of the cost. But it was their smart positioning that truly set them apart. Rather than competing on the quality or innovation of the razor itself, Dollar Shave Club focused on convenience and value. Their subscription model offered customers an easy, hassle-free way to get quality razors without paying for the unnecessary bells and whistles.

The brand's viral launch video, featuring its irreverent humor and direct messaging, was a masterclass in positioning. The video spoke directly to the frustrations of male consumers fed up with high razor prices and overcomplicated products. It framed the brand as a simple, no-nonsense alternative to overpriced giants like Gillette. This positioning resonated with men who didn't want to pay premium prices for minor features they didn't need.

What made Dollar Shave Club even more compelling was their ability to make their customers feel smart for choosing them. By offering a high-value product without the high price tag, Dollar Shave Club created a narrative that consumers were making a savvy choice by subscribing. They weren't just saving money — they were opting out of the traditional, overpriced system.

The takeaway: Disruption through positioning

Both Uber and Dollar Shave Club succeeded because they didn't just introduce a product — they introduced a new way of thinking about existing problems. Uber repositioned transportation as a personal, tech-enabled experience, while Dollar Shave Club redefined the razor-buying experience as affordable and hassle-free.

By understanding their customers' frustrations and positioning their brands as solutions to those pain points, both companies created compelling narratives that stuck. Uber made getting from point A to point B easier and more efficient, while Dollar Shave Club simplified an everyday purchase and made it more affordable.

The lesson here is clear: smart positioning doesn't just differentiate a brand; it can disrupt an entire industry. By focusing on solving the right problem and communicating that solution effectively, your brand can carve out a space where it not only competes — but leads.

Next, we'll explore how to maintain your position through consistency across all channels and customer touchpoints, ensuring your brand stays top of mind.

CHAPTER 07

CONSISTENCY IS QUEEN

Trust through consistency

Trust is the bedrock of any successful brand, and the fastest way to build it is through consistency. When a brand is consistent—whether in its messaging, product quality, or customer service—it creates a sense of reliability. Customers know what to expect, and over time, that predictability fosters trust. On the other hand, a brand that frequently changes its tone, experience, or offerings risks confusing its audience and undermining confidence.

Consistency isn't just about doing the same thing over and over—it's about delivering a cohesive and unified experience that reflects your brand's values every single time.

Consistency in messaging

One of the most important aspects of building trust through consistency is your brand's messaging. Your voice, tone, and communication should remain steady across all platforms—whether it's a social media post, an email campaign, or a billboard. When your message shifts too much, it creates doubt in your customers' minds about what you stand for.

Consider a brand like Ikea. Their messaging is always clear, approachable, and focused on the idea of "affordable home solutions." Whether you're watching an Ikea commercial or reading their catalog, you know that the message will consistently revolve around accessible, stylish furniture for everyone. This creates a strong brand identity that customers can rely on and trust.

Product and service consistency

Consistency isn't just about words—it's about the experience your customers have with your product or service. If a customer buys your product expecting a certain level of quality, and that quality fluctuates, trust is immediately broken. Brands that consistently deliver on their promises create loyalty because customers know they can depend on them.

Apple is a strong example of this. Year after year, customers return to buy the latest iPhone not just because of new features, but because they trust Apple's track record of delivering high-quality, intuitive technology. Apple's consistency in both design and performance has built a sense of reliability that keeps customers coming back.

The impact of inconsistent experiences

A lack of consistency can have damaging effects on your brand. Imagine a coffee shop where your drink is perfect one day but disappointing the next. You quickly lose confidence, and even if the coffee is great sometimes, the inconsistency drives you to seek out a more reliable alternative.

When customers experience inconsistency, they begin to question the brand. Is the company cutting corners? Are they unable to maintain standards? Once doubt creeps in, trust erodes—and with it, loyalty.

The power of routines

When a brand is consistent, it often becomes a part of the customer's routine. People are creatures of habit, and when they find a brand that consistently meets their needs, it integrates into their lives. This kind of dependability creates not just trust, but loyalty that can last for years.

Think about Netflix. Their consistently high level of service—easy access to a vast library of content, personalized recommendations, and a seamless streaming experience—has made Netflix a staple in millions of households. People don't think twice about their subscription because they know exactly what they're getting. Netflix has earned their trust by reliably delivering entertainment without hiccups.

Consistency as a trust-building tool

The power of consistency lies in its ability to make customers feel secure in their choices. When they know exactly what they're getting every time they engage with your brand, trust becomes second nature. Consistency reassures customers that they won't be disappointed, which is why it's one of the most critical elements in building long-term loyalty.

Next, we'll explore how inconsistency can destroy even the most beloved brands and why maintaining a steady presence across all channels is crucial for survival.

How inconsistency kills brands

Consistency is often the unsung hero of brand success, but inconsistency? That's the silent killer. It can slowly erode trust, create confusion, and ultimately push customers away. When brands don't maintain a steady presence—whether in their messaging, product quality, or customer experience—they risk becoming unreliable in the eyes of their audience. And once trust is broken, it's incredibly difficult to rebuild.

Inconsistent brands fail to create the strong foundation needed to develop long-term loyalty. Instead, they leave customers guessing, which can result in frustration and lost sales.

Confusing messaging alienates customers

One of the most common ways inconsistency kills a brand is through mixed messaging. When your tone, voice, or value proposition changes frequently, customers become confused about what your brand stands for. A brand that appears serious and formal one day, but playful and irreverent the next, will struggle to build a coherent identity.

Take the case of Gap in 2010. The brand attempted to change its iconic logo to something more modern and minimalistic, but it was met with backlash from customers who identified with the original. The abrupt shift confused loyal customers, leading to negative publicity and a quick reversal of the decision. Inconsistent brand presentation not only damaged trust, but it also signaled a lack of confidence in their identity.

Inconsistent quality breaks trust

Customers expect the same experience every time they interact with your brand. When product quality or service delivery is inconsistent, it sends a signal that the brand is unreliable. Even a single bad experience can make customers hesitate before coming back, and frequent inconsistencies will push them to seek alternatives.

Look at Blackberry, once a giant in the smartphone market. Over time, the company's focus on its core strengths wavered as it attempted to catch up with competitors like Apple and Samsung. The inconsistent roll-out of new models and features alienated their once-loyal customer base, and Blackberry's decline was swift. What was once a brand associated with cutting-edge technology and reliability became a shadow of its former self, largely due to inconsistent quality and innovation.

Conflicting brand values create distrust

If your brand's actions don't align with its stated values, customers quickly lose trust. This form of inconsistency is especially damaging in an era where consumers are more conscious of brand authenticity. When a brand's public image doesn't match what they deliver behind the scenes, customers feel deceived.

Take the infamous example of Volkswagen's emissions scandal. For years, Volkswagen positioned itself as an environmentally friendly car manufacturer, only for it to be revealed that they had been manipulating emissions tests. This shocking inconsistency between the brand's values and its actions shattered trust and resulted in massive fines, lawsuits, and damage to their reputation that took years to recover from.

Why inconsistency opens doors for competitors

Inconsistency doesn't just frustrate your existing customers — it creates opportunities for your competitors. When customers can't rely on your brand, they start looking elsewhere, and competitors that offer a more dependable experience will gladly swoop in.

Brands that remain steady in their messaging, product delivery, and values provide customers with a sense of security. On the other hand, brands that can't seem to get it right leave a vacuum, one that competitors can easily fill by offering a clearer, more reliable alternative.

The bottom line: Consistency is trust

At its core, inconsistency undermines the very thing brands work hard to build: trust. A brand that constantly shifts its identity, messaging, or product quality isn't one that customers can rely on. Without consistency, even the most well-established brands can falter, losing the loyalty they've worked so hard to earn.

Next, we'll dive into examples of brands that lost their way through inconsistency, and how the fallout affected their long-term success.

Brands that lost their way

Even the most iconic brands can fall from grace if they lose sight of what made them successful in the first place. When brands lose their way—whether through inconsistency, losing touch with their audience, or making misguided decisions—they often face an uphill battle to regain their former status. It's a reminder that no brand, no matter how powerful, is immune to the consequences of losing focus.

Blockbuster: Failure to adapt

Blockbuster was once a giant in the home entertainment industry, with thousands of stores worldwide. At its peak, Blockbuster was the go-to place for renting movies, and its name was synonymous with a Friday night spent browsing VHS tapes and DVDs. However, Blockbuster's downfall was rooted in its failure to adapt to changing market conditions and customer preferences.

As streaming services like Netflix began to emerge, Blockbuster stuck to its traditional brick-and-mortar model. Rather than innovating or embracing the shift to digital, Blockbuster remained stagnant, still focused on late fees and physical rentals while customers were shifting to on-demand streaming. Their reluctance to evolve and inconsistent response to the changing landscape left a massive gap, which Netflix quickly filled.

By the time Blockbuster tried to launch its own streaming service, it was too late. The brand had lost its relevance, and customers had already moved on. Blockbuster's story serves as a cautionary tale of how losing sight of market trends and consumer behavior can lead to an irreversible decline.

Yahoo: From internet pioneer to also-ran

Yahoo was once a dominant force in the early days of the internet, leading the charge in search, news, email, and even early social networking. Yet, over time, Yahoo's inability to focus and its scattered approach to business led to its downfall.

Yahoo's leadership made a series of inconsistent decisions, acquiring businesses that didn't align with their core mission or focus. From the failed acquisition of Tumblr to missing the opportunity to buy Google, Yahoo struggled with direction. Their strategy seemed to shift every few years, chasing trends rather than setting them.

As competitors like Google doubled down on innovation and consistency in their services, Yahoo floundered. Their once-dominant search engine fell behind, and their scattered approach to media and technology left users unsure of what Yahoo truly stood for. Inconsistent leadership and direction caused Yahoo to lose relevance in the tech world, eventually leading to its acquisition by Verizon at a fraction of its former value.

Myspace: The social giant that crumbled

Myspace was the first major social media platform, and for a while, it dominated the social networking scene. In its early years, Myspace gave users the freedom to customize their profiles, connect with friends, and discover new music, becoming a cultural phenomenon.

But Myspace lost its way when it failed to innovate in the face of emerging competition from Facebook. While Facebook focused on simplicity, user privacy, and a clean design, Myspace remained cluttered and inconsistent in its user experience. Its platform became harder to navigate, and as it bombarded users with ads, it felt increasingly out of touch with what its audience wanted.

As Facebook grew, Myspace's inability to stay focused on improving user experience caused it to rapidly lose ground. The brand's inconsistency in adapting to user needs and technological advances led to its swift decline, and today, Myspace is little more than a footnote in the history of social media.

The lessons learned

The common thread in these brands' downfalls is inconsistency—whether it was a failure to adapt to market changes, poor leadership decisions, or a misalignment with customer expectations. Blockbuster, Yahoo, and Myspace all show that brands that lose their way often find it impossible to recover, especially when more consistent and focused competitors are ready to take their place.

Staying consistent in vision, mission, and customer experience is crucial for long-term success. Brands that remain adaptable but consistent in their core values are far more likely to thrive in an ever-changing marketplace.

Next, we'll explore how brands can ensure consistency across every customer touchpoint to build trust and maintain their position in the market.

Ensuring consistency across channels

In today's omnichannel world, customers interact with brands in multiple ways—through websites, social media, physical stores, customer service, and more. Each interaction is a touchpoint that shapes their overall perception of the brand. If a brand feels cohesive across all these channels, it reinforces trust and reliability. But if there are inconsistencies in the experience, it can lead to confusion and erode that trust.

Consistency across channels doesn't just happen—it requires careful planning and coordination. Whether a customer is scrolling through your Instagram feed or talking to a customer service representative, the brand's voice, values, and quality must stay aligned.

Unified messaging

The first step to ensuring consistency is delivering a unified message across all communication platforms. Whether it's through a social media post, an email campaign, or a printed ad, the tone, style, and core message should always reflect the same values. A fragmented message can leave customers uncertain about what your brand stands for.

Take Coca-Cola, for example. Whether you encounter their brand on a billboard, in-store packaging, or through an online campaign, the message of happiness and togetherness shines through. They maintain a consistent tone—positive, refreshing, and universal. No matter where a customer interacts with Coca-Cola, they're met with the same message, creating a reliable and reassuring brand experience.

Visual consistency

Visual consistency is equally important in maintaining a strong brand identity. Your logo, color scheme, fonts, and overall design should remain consistent across all platforms. When customers see these visual cues, they immediately recognize your brand, and that recognition builds trust.

Look at Nike. Whether you're looking at their website, a social media post, or a physical store, the iconic swoosh and the "Just Do It" slogan are always front and center. Their design is bold and clean, ensuring that no matter where you encounter Nike, you instantly recognize the brand. This visual consistency reinforces Nike's message of performance, empowerment, and athletic excellence.

Consistent customer service

Beyond visuals and messaging, consistency in customer service is crucial for maintaining trust. If customers have vastly different experiences when interacting with your brand—whether online, in-store, or over the phone—it creates doubt about the reliability of your brand as a whole.

Consider Amazon's approach to customer service. Across all channels—whether a customer is seeking help through live chat, email, or over the phone—Amazon delivers quick, efficient, and solution-oriented service. This consistency has helped build Amazon's reputation for excellent customer care, making them a trusted brand that customers return to again and again.

Adapting to the platform while maintaining core identity

Consistency doesn't mean being identical on every platform. Each channel has its nuances, and brands must adapt their approach to fit the medium. However, the core identity and messaging should always remain the same.

For instance, while a company might use a more formal tone in email communications, their social media presence may allow for a more casual, engaging tone. The key is to ensure that the underlying message and brand identity remain intact. Take Starbucks, for example. On Instagram, they might share vibrant, colorful posts celebrating seasonal drinks, while their website maintains a clean, polished tone. The messaging adapts to the platform, but the core identity—community, creativity, and warmth—remains consistent.

Coordinating internal teams for external consistency

Ensuring consistency across channels requires a unified internal effort. Marketing, sales, customer service, and even product development teams need to be aligned in their understanding of the brand's values and voice. When teams are siloed or disconnected, it often results in mixed messages or inconsistent customer experiences.

Brands that excel at this, like Apple, ensure that every department is on the same page when it comes to delivering a consistent customer experience. Whether it's the design team working on packaging, the marketing team crafting campaigns, or the customer service department addressing issues, they all reinforce the same values of innovation, simplicity, and quality.

The bottom line: A seamless brand experience

In a world where customers engage with brands across multiple touchpoints, consistency is non-negotiable. Brands that create a seamless, unified experience across all channels not only build trust but also enhance customer loyalty. Each interaction, whether visual, verbal, or experiential, should feel like a piece of the larger brand puzzle—cohesive, reliable, and instantly recognizable.

By delivering consistency across channels, you show customers that your brand is stable, dependable, and worthy of their loyalty.

Up next, we'll begin exploring the digital landscape and how brands can build strong, consistent digital-first strategies in a world that increasingly values online interactions.

CHAPTER 08

DIGITAL-FIRST BRANDING

Omnichannel without being annoying

Connecting with customers across multiple platforms is a must, but there's a fine line between engaging them and overwhelming them. While an omnichannel approach is essential for maintaining a presence where your audience lives—whether that's online, in-store, through social media, or email—it's equally important to make sure your brand is adding value and not just creating noise.

The real challenge? How to show up consistently across channels without coming across as intrusive or pushy. It's about creating a seamless experience that feels natural, not forced.

Be where your audience is, not everywhere

One common mistake brands make with omnichannel marketing is assuming they need to be everywhere. It's tempting to try to hit every platform—email, social, text messages, apps—but spreading yourself too thin often leads to a disjointed and, frankly, annoying experience for your audience.

Take Everlane as an example. The clothing brand doesn't bombard customers with unnecessary emails or texts. Instead, they focus on platforms that truly engage their audience. Their Instagram presence is strong and visual, while their email communications focus on transparency and product updates that feel informative rather than intrusive. This creates a sense of balance, ensuring their audience never feels overwhelmed.

The key is identifying the channels where your customers are most active and creating meaningful touchpoints there, rather than trying to be on every possible platform.

Respect your customer's time

Nobody likes to feel bombarded by notifications and messages. When brands over-communicate—whether that's through daily emails or constant push notifications—they risk turning customers off. Instead of strengthening the relationship, they end up driving customers away.

One way to avoid this is by giving customers control. Let them choose how often they want to hear from you, and through which channels. Providing these options makes your communication feel respectful and tailored. Patagonia, for instance, allows customers to set preferences for how often they receive emails, ensuring that they're reaching people on their own terms.

This approach keeps your brand top-of-mind without becoming an annoyance.

Create a seamless, cohesive experience

An omnichannel strategy shouldn't feel like you're interacting with different versions of the same brand on each platform. Whether a customer is browsing your website, visiting your store, or engaging with you on social media, the experience should feel cohesive and connected.

Nordstrom has perfected this. Their in-store and online shopping experiences are tightly integrated. Customers can check online to see what's available in-store, order items for in-store pickup, or even return online purchases to a physical location. Each touchpoint builds on the next, creating a fluid and convenient shopping journey. This seamless experience strengthens the customer relationship without bombarding them with irrelevant messaging or offers.

Personalization without overstepping

While personalization is a key part of any omnichannel strategy, it's easy to cross the line into feeling invasive. Customers appreciate personalized recommendations and offers when they're timely and relevant, but too much personal data use can feel like a breach of privacy.

Spotify does an excellent job of personalizing their platform without overstepping. Their personalized playlists and recommendations feel like a helpful part of the user experience, enhancing rather than interrupting. It's a careful balance: making customers feel understood without making them feel like they're being watched too closely.

The takeaway here is to use customer data wisely—don't over-personalize to the point of making people uncomfortable.

Keep your communication relevant

There's no faster way to lose your audience than by sending irrelevant messages. An effective omnichannel strategy isn't just about maintaining presence—it's about ensuring that every interaction delivers value. Irrelevant or repetitive messaging is the fastest way to annoy and alienate customers.

Sephora excels in keeping their communications relevant. The beauty brand's omnichannel strategy is focused on delivering value, whether it's through personalized product recommendations, exclusive offers, or tailored content. By keeping their messaging aligned with customer preferences and behavior, Sephora remains an engaging presence without feeling like a nagging one.

Less is more

At the end of the day, being omnipresent doesn't mean overwhelming your customers with constant touchpoints. Sometimes, less is more. Strategic, well-timed interactions are far more effective than simply trying to be everywhere, all the time.

A thoughtful approach to omnichannel communication means finding the balance between visibility and value. When done right, you're not just a brand that exists on multiple platforms—you're a brand that customers actually want to engage with.

Next, we'll explore how brands can navigate the challenges of balancing algorithms and authenticity, ensuring that their digital presence doesn't lose its human touch.

The influencer dilemma

In times where everyone is vying for attention, influencers have become powerful allies in helping brands reach their audience. But with so many influencers promoting similar products, how do you ensure that your brand stands out? The challenge isn't just finding an influencer with a massive following—it's about choosing partners who can truly differentiate your brand from the sea of bland competitors.

The real dilemma? Influencers can amplify your brand, but if they're not carefully chosen, they can also dilute your uniqueness.

Differentiation through authenticity

Choosing an influencer who fits your brand's identity is crucial for maintaining differentiation. It's not enough to simply work with someone who has a large audience—you need someone whose values, tone, and lifestyle align with your brand's vision. Otherwise, your message gets lost among all the other products and partnerships that influencers are pushing.

Consider skincare brand Drunk Elephant. Instead of working with influencers who promote any and every beauty product, Drunk Elephant chooses influencers who are passionate about clean beauty and transparency. By aligning with influencers who truly care about their message, Drunk Elephant differentiates itself as a brand that stands by its values, even in a crowded space.

Influencers as a tool for brand differentiation

Influencers can help your brand break away from the generic and mundane if they're used strategically. Working with the same influencers as your competitors won't set you apart. Instead, consider collaborating with micro-influencers or niche voices who speak to a highly specific audience that resonates with your brand's unique positioning.

Outdoor clothing brand Fjällräven, for example, partners with influencers who are deeply embedded in the adventure and sustainability communities. These influencers aren't just promoting products—they're showcasing a lifestyle that aligns with Fjällräven's commitment to quality and sustainability. By working with influencers who have deep credibility in their niche, Fjällräven effectively differentiates itself from other outdoor brands that take a more mainstream approach.

Avoiding the trap of sameness

One of the biggest dangers of influencer marketing is falling into the trap of sameness. When influencers endorse a dozen different brands in a short period, their posts start to blur together, and the authenticity fades. As a brand, you risk being just another face in the crowd, especially if the influencer's audience sees them promoting too many competing products.

To stand out, your brand must be intentional about how it partners with influencers. Rather than quick, one-off deals, long-term partnerships create deeper, more meaningful content that aligns with your brand's story. Long-term influencer collaborations show that your brand is invested in the relationship, which can help to differentiate you from others using shallow, transactional approaches.

Standing out with purpose-driven influencers

A powerful way to differentiate your brand through influencer marketing is by partnering with purpose-driven influencers who have a genuine passion for your mission. In a world where customers are increasingly looking for brands that stand for something, aligning your brand with influencers who share your values is a strong way to cut through the noise.

Toms, the socially conscious shoe brand, stands out by working with influencers who genuinely care about social impact. These influencers don't just promote the product; they advocate for the causes that Toms supports. This alignment with socially conscious influencers helps Toms reinforce its differentiation as a brand that blends commerce with social good, ensuring that they remain distinct in a market full of generic footwear options.

Making influence a key part of your differentiation strategy

When used thoughtfully, influencers can play a major role in setting your brand apart from the rest. The key is not in using influencers for the sake of visibility, but in using them to help tell your unique story. Whether it's through carefully chosen micro-influencers, purpose-driven partnerships, or long-term collaborations, influencers can help bring your differentiation strategy to life—provided they align with the core values that make your brand special.

The lesson? Influencers aren't just a marketing tool—they're a reflection of your brand's identity. Choose wisely, and they'll help you rise above the sea of sameness.

Next, we'll explore how to craft a digital-first strategy that not only keeps your brand relevant but also amplifies its distinct voice in the online world.

Crafting a digital-first strategy

Being present in the digital world is no longer optional—it's essential. But simply existing online won't set your brand apart. To differentiate in a space that's increasingly crowded, your digital-first strategy needs to be more than just about showing up. It needs to be about standing out, offering a unique and engaging experience that feels authentic and aligns with your brand's core values.

A strong digital-first strategy is built around your brand's distinctive voice and the value you bring to the table. It's about creating an online presence that doesn't just follow trends but establishes your brand as a leader in your space.

Aligning digital with your brand's unique DNA

The first step in crafting a digital-first strategy that stands out is ensuring that your online presence reflects what makes your brand different. Your website, social media, email campaigns, and all digital touchpoints should clearly communicate who you are and what sets you apart from the competition.

Take Warby Parker, the eyewear brand that revolutionized the industry with its direct-to-consumer model. From the beginning, their digital strategy wasn't just about selling glasses online—it was about making the process seamless, affordable, and enjoyable. Their "Home Try-On" program, paired with a clean, user-friendly website, redefined how people buy eyewear and set Warby Parker apart as a brand that values convenience and customer experience. Their digital-first approach aligned perfectly with their commitment to simplicity and transparency.

Personalization without losing integrity

The rise of personalization in digital marketing has made it easier than ever to tailor experiences for individual customers. However, brands that overdo personalization run the risk of feeling invasive rather than engaging. To stand out digitally, personalization must be done thoughtfully, ensuring it enhances the customer experience without crossing into uncomfortable territory.

Spotify does this well. Their algorithms tailor music recommendations for each user, but rather than feeling robotic, Spotify's approach is framed as a way to enhance each listener's experience. The personalized "Discover Weekly" playlist is a great example of how Spotify uses data to create a unique, enjoyable experience without sacrificing authenticity. This kind of personalization reinforces Spotify's differentiation as a music streaming service that "gets you."

Innovation over imitation

In the digital space, it's easy to be reactive—jumping on trends that seem to be gaining traction. However, real differentiation comes from leading the charge, not following it. Brands that craft a digital-first strategy centered on innovation are the ones that stand out, offering their audience something they can't get anywhere else.

Glossier, for example, didn't just build a website to sell beauty products; they created a community-driven digital ecosystem. Their platform encourages users to share their beauty routines, post reviews, and engage with one another. By prioritizing user-generated content and community interaction, Glossier made their digital presence more than just a shop—it became a space where people feel connected. This level of innovation in the beauty industry helped Glossier rise above competitors who merely focus on product features.

The importance of content that matters

Content lies at the heart of every digital-first strategy. But with the sheer volume of content being produced, standing out requires more than just pushing out endless blogs, posts, and videos. It's about creating content that actually resonates with your audience and strengthens your brand's identity.

Patagonia uses its digital platforms not just to sell clothes but to advocate for environmental causes. Their content is focused on their mission—raising awareness about sustainability and the environment, while offering practical ways for customers to get involved. This approach differentiates Patagonia from other outdoor brands, making their content not just informative, but meaningful and purpose-driven.

Your digital-first strategy should ensure that every piece of content—whether it's a blog post, video, or email—is a reflection of what makes your brand different. It's not about volume; it's about impact.

Seamless integration across channels

A successful digital-first strategy isn't about being present on every platform—it's about creating a seamless, integrated experience across the platforms that matter most to your audience. Your website, social media, and email campaigns should feel like parts of a cohesive whole, working together to tell your brand's story in a way that makes sense.

Nike's digital ecosystem is a masterclass in seamless integration. Whether you're interacting with them via their app, website, or social media, the experience is cohesive and aligned. The Nike Training Club app, for instance, doesn't just sell products—it offers workouts, fitness tips, and exclusive content that enhances the user experience. This kind of integration ensures that no matter how a customer engages with Nike, the brand experience remains consistent and immersive.

The road ahead

Building a digital-first strategy is about more than simply leveraging technology—it's about differentiating your brand in a space where everyone else is trying to do the same. Focus on innovation, create meaningful content, and always align your online presence with your brand's core identity. The brands that master this balance are the ones that lead the conversation, not just join it.

Next, we'll dive into case studies of how Warby Parker and Glossier have built digital-first strategies that set them apart from their competitors, making them leaders in their respective industries.

Case studies: Warby Parker and Glossier

As seen, differentiation is key to standing out in the digital landscape, and brands like Warby Parker and Glossier have mastered the art of crafting digital-first strategies that don't just follow trends—they set them. These two companies have redefined their industries by using innovative approaches that go beyond simply selling products. They've built unique, engaging digital ecosystems that reflect their brand identities and deliver memorable experiences to their customers.

Warby Parker: Reinventing eyewear with a digital twist

Warby Parker entered the eyewear market with a simple but disruptive goal: make high-quality, stylish glasses affordable. But what truly set them apart was how they built their brand around a digital-first strategy. From the start, Warby Parker understood that the key to differentiation wasn't just offering lower prices—it was about transforming how people bought glasses.

Instead of opening physical stores, they launched as an online retailer, a bold move in a space where customers traditionally wanted to try on products in person. To address this, Warby Parker introduced their innovative "Home Try-On" program, allowing customers to select five frames online and have them shipped for free to try at home. This unique digital-first approach removed the hassle from the buying process and gave customers confidence in making an online purchase.

Warby Parker's website and app are designed to make the process seamless, from browsing to ordering, and their use of online prescription management and virtual try-ons has further pushed them ahead of competitors. By focusing on convenience and using technology to make the experience smoother, Warby Parker differentiates itself from traditional eyewear retailers stuck in brick-and-mortar models.

Moreover, Warby Parker leverages data to continually improve its offerings, creating a personalized shopping experience that feels tailored to each individual. Their ability to integrate an exceptional online experience with a growing network of physical stores shows that a digital-first strategy doesn't have to be digital-only. The result? Warby Parker stands out as a brand that doesn't just sell glasses—it redefines the eyewear experience.

Glossier: Building a community, not just a brand

Glossier didn't just disrupt the beauty industry—they reimagined how beauty brands could build relationships with their customers in a digital-first world. From day one, Glossier was built on a foundation of direct engagement, creating a brand that speaks with its customers, not at them.

What truly sets Glossier apart is its community-driven approach. The brand used social media not only as a marketing tool but as a way to foster genuine conversations. Glossier's digital presence feels more like a dialogue than a sales pitch. Their Instagram page, for example, is filled with user-generated content, featuring real customers using their products in everyday life. This focus on the authentic voice of the customer helps Glossier stand out from competitors that rely on celebrity endorsements or overly polished campaigns.

Glossier's website design also reflects its customer-centric philosophy. The site is simple, user-friendly, and encourages engagement with features like reviews, tutorials, and real-life product applications. By keeping things minimal and focusing on usability, Glossier makes shopping online easy and personal.

Another factor that differentiates Glossier is its use of data. Every product launch is informed by customer feedback collected through social media and surveys. The brand actively listens to what customers want, using that information to develop new products and improve existing ones. This feedback loop ensures that Glossier remains hyper-relevant to its audience, staying ahead of trends rather than reacting to them.

But Glossier's digital-first success isn't just about engagement. It's about creating a brand experience that makes every customer feel like they're part of an exclusive community. Whether through digital platforms or their physical retail experiences, Glossier maintains a consistent focus on what matters most: the customer's voice. This strategy is a big reason Glossier has managed to stand out in the ultra-competitive beauty industry.

What we can learn from Warby Parker and Glossier

Both brands demonstrate that crafting a digital-first strategy is not about chasing the latest technology or being on every platform. It's about understanding your audience and creating an experience that makes your brand stand out from competitors. Warby Parker disrupted the traditional retail model by making buying glasses online seamless and fun, while Glossier built a community-first beauty brand by putting their customers at the center of everything they do.

The lesson? A successful digital-first strategy is about using technology to enhance your unique brand story, not letting it overshadow your identity. Warby Parker and Glossier's focus on personalization, community, and customer experience sets them apart in industries filled with brands trying to do the same thing.

Next, we'll explore how to maintain consistency in your digital-first approach and ensure that your brand doesn't lose sight of what makes it unique, even as you grow and adapt.

CHAPTER 09

STANDING OUT IN SAMENESS

Adding value, not noise

With so much content vying for attention, brands have two choices: contribute to the noise or provide something genuinely valuable. The brands that stand out focus not on simply being louder, but on offering their audience something meaningful—something that solves a problem, sparks interest, or enhances their lives. The real goal isn't just visibility; it's creating an experience that resonates and adds value.

Quality over quantity

Many brands fall into the trap of thinking that more content equals more success. They flood social media feeds, email inboxes, and websites with constant updates, posts, and promotions, hoping to stay top-of-mind. But this approach often leads to diminishing returns. When customers are inundated with too many messages, they tune out—unless those messages offer something that captures their interest.

Apple stands as a prime example of a brand that focuses on quality over quantity. Instead of bombarding users with frequent updates, they are selective with their communication, making each message impactful. Their product announcements, campaigns, and content are thoughtfully crafted and highly anticipated. By focusing on creating fewer, high-impact interactions, Apple has built a brand that commands attention, rather than one that fades into the background.

Solving problems, not selling products

One of the key ways to add value is by focusing on what your audience truly needs. Brands that differentiate themselves don't just push products—they offer solutions. When you position your brand as a helpful resource or guide, your content becomes something customers actively seek out, rather than something they ignore.

For example, Duolingo, the language-learning app, provides value by offering a free and engaging way for users to learn new languages. Their content and platform aren't just focused on selling premium memberships—they're about making language learning accessible to everyone. By focusing on solving a real problem for their users, Duolingo has created a brand that feels indispensable rather than just another service.

Engaging with intent

Another way to add value is by being intentional with engagement. Rather than aiming for mass interaction, successful brands focus on targeted, meaningful conversations with their audience. Whether through personalized email campaigns or responsive social media engagement, brands that truly connect with their customers create deeper relationships and foster loyalty.

REI, the outdoor gear company, does this exceptionally well. Their campaigns are designed to speak directly to the adventurous, eco-conscious audience they serve. REI's "Opt Outside" campaign isn't just about selling gear; it's about encouraging people to get outdoors and experience nature. This initiative adds real value by aligning with their customers' values and passions, making the brand feel more like a partner in their lifestyle rather than just another retailer.

Avoiding the noise trap

It's tempting to adopt every new platform and trend in an effort to stay relevant, but adding value means knowing when not to speak. Brands that try to be everywhere often spread themselves thin, diluting their message and losing focus. True differentiation comes from selecting the right channels, creating the right content, and engaging in ways that matter to your audience.

Minimalism isn't just a design choice—it's a strategy. Take Basecamp, the project management software company. Basecamp deliberately avoids unnecessary complexity, both in their product and their marketing. Their messaging is simple, clear, and direct, focusing on helping customers get work done without distractions. By refusing to add unnecessary features or content, Basecamp provides a clean, valuable experience that cuts through the noise of overly complicated software competitors.

A brand that matters

At the end of the day, the brands that thrive are the ones that focus on value first. It's not about pushing out as much content as possible—it's about crafting experiences and messages that truly resonate with the audience. Whether through solving problems, creating community, or simply being selective with communication, brands that prioritize value over volume stand out in a world full of noise.

Next, we'll explore why boldness wins in branding, and how taking calculated risks can lead to meaningful differentiation.

Why boldness wins

Playing it safe rarely leads to differentiation. Brands that are willing to take risks, push boundaries, and embrace bold strategies are the ones that truly stand out. Boldness isn't about being loud or flashy—it's about making decisions that reflect confidence, creativity, and a willingness to break from convention. In a marketplace where many brands play it safe, boldness is often the key to cutting through the noise and leaving a lasting impression.

Standing out with a clear point of view

One of the most powerful ways to be bold is by having a strong, unapologetic point of view. Brands that succeed in differentiating themselves are often the ones that aren't afraid to take a stand, even if it means polarizing some customers. A clear point of view shows confidence, and in a world full of neutrality, boldness becomes memorable.

Ben & Jerry's is a prime example of a brand that doesn't shy away from taking a stand on social and political issues. Whether advocating for climate change action or supporting racial justice movements, Ben & Jerry's uses its platform to speak out on issues that matter to the brand and its audience. By taking bold, sometimes controversial positions, the company has built a strong emotional connection with like-minded customers, reinforcing their differentiation in the market.

Bold products and services

Boldness can also manifest in product development. Brands that dare to innovate or reimagine their offerings often gain a competitive edge. This doesn't always mean introducing cutting-edge technology or inventing entirely new products—it could be as simple as rethinking an established category in a way that makes customers look twice.

Take Dyson, for instance. When they entered the vacuum cleaner market, the industry was dominated by traditional designs and standard technologies. Dyson disrupted the market by developing a vacuum that used cyclone technology, eliminating the need for bags and filters. This bold move not only introduced a revolutionary product but also positioned Dyson as a leader in innovation, challenging the conventions of a relatively stagnant industry.

Creating bold experiences

Boldness isn't limited to the products you create—it extends to the experiences you offer. Brands that think creatively about how to engage customers in unexpected ways can carve out a unique space in the market.

Consider Red Bull. Beyond selling energy drinks, Red Bull has positioned itself as a brand that represents extreme sports, adventure, and pushing limits. Through their bold sponsorships of events like the Red Bull Air Race and their involvement in extreme sports like skydiving and motor racing, they've created a brand experience that's synonymous with adrenaline and excitement. This focus on bold experiences, rather than just selling a product, has allowed Red Bull to maintain its strong position as a leader in its category.

The risk of playing it safe

Many brands hesitate to take bold actions because they fear alienating customers or making mistakes. But playing it safe often results in blending in with everyone else, which is far more dangerous for long-term success. Brands that are too cautious can easily become forgettable, lost in a sea of competitors that offer similar products and messaging.

Blockbuster's reluctance to adapt to digital streaming is a classic example of playing it too safe. While competitors like Netflix were embracing new technology and business models, Blockbuster stuck to its tried-and-true formula of physical rentals. This cautious approach ultimately led to their downfall, as they failed to take bold, decisive action when the market was changing around them.

Boldness builds emotional connections

When a brand takes bold steps, it often evokes strong emotional responses from its audience. Whether it's excitement, admiration, or even surprise, these emotions can create a deeper connection with customers than a brand that sticks to a more traditional, cautious approach.

For instance, LEGO's decision to launch the LEGO Ideas platform, where fans can submit their own designs to be turned into official sets, was a bold move that shifted some control from the brand to its customers. This initiative gave fans a sense of ownership and investment in the brand, strengthening their emotional connection with LEGO while differentiating it from competitors.

Making boldness a part of your brand identity

For boldness to work as a differentiator, it needs to be authentic. Bold actions that feel forced or inauthentic can backfire, causing customers to lose trust. But when boldness is rooted in your brand's values and mission, it creates a compelling narrative that resonates deeply with your audience.

The brands that lead with boldness show the courage to take risks and the confidence to stand by their decisions. These are the brands that break through the noise, challenge the status quo, and create lasting impact.

Next, we'll explore how niche audiences can be a secret weapon for differentiation, and why focusing on smaller, more targeted groups often leads to bigger rewards.

Niche audiences: Your secret weapon

Many brands chase the broadest audience possible, but those that focus on niche markets often find a faster path to standing out. Catering to a well-defined, specific group creates stronger connections and deeper loyalty, giving your brand a distinct position that larger competitors may struggle to achieve. When your brand speaks directly to a niche audience, you're not just meeting their needs—you're becoming essential to them.

Why niches matter

Targeting a specific audience allows you to develop products, services, and messaging that resonate on a personal level. When you tailor your brand to serve the unique needs of a niche, it signals that you truly understand and care about your audience. This kind of focus creates loyalty that mass-market brands often miss.

Take Oatly, the oat milk brand. By zeroing in on health-conscious consumers and those focused on sustainability, Oatly didn't try to appeal to everyone. Instead, it connected deeply with a smaller group whose values aligned with the brand's environmental and health-focused messaging. This focus helped Oatly rise above competitors in the crowded plant-based milk market.

Becoming indispensable

Serving a niche audience means offering something they can't easily find elsewhere, making your brand feel irreplaceable. Niche audiences tend to be underserved by mainstream brands, and when you fill that gap with products or experiences tailored specifically for them, you set your brand apart.

Aesop, the luxury skincare brand, has built its success by targeting customers who care deeply about natural ingredients and minimalist design. Instead of appealing to the mass-market beauty crowd, Aesop created a loyal following within this specific segment. By focusing on a niche, the brand didn't need to appeal to everyone — they became a must-have for their core audience.

Small audiences, big loyalty

Though niche audiences may be smaller, they often show higher levels of engagement and loyalty. These customers are more likely to become advocates for your brand, turning their deep connection into word-of-mouth promotion. Focusing on a dedicated audience allows your brand to feel exclusive and special, creating a strong emotional bond that larger competitors struggle to achieve.

Rather than attempting to serve everyone, niche brands focus on being irreplaceable to the few — and that can lead to greater long-term success.

Next, we'll dive into the critical choice brands must make between standing out or fading away, and how differentiation is no longer optional but necessary for survival.

Differentiation or extinction

Brands today face a simple reality: those that fail to stand out risk fading into irrelevance. With consumers flooded by endless choices, being average or just "good enough" won't secure loyalty or attention. The brands that thrive are those that make a bold statement, offering something unique that resonates with their audience. The alternative is extinction, as undifferentiated brands get lost in the crowd and slowly disappear.

Why differentiation is critical

It's not about being different for the sake of it, but about offering something distinct that speaks directly to your audience's needs and values. Brands that succeed create lasting connections and build trust through their uniqueness, while those that don't simply blend in with countless others, becoming forgettable.

Take Blockbuster, for example. At its height, the company dominated the video rental market, but it failed to innovate when streaming services like Netflix emerged. Blockbuster's inability to differentiate in a changing landscape led to its downfall. Netflix, on the other hand, took bold steps by offering a new way to consume content, which allowed it to thrive while Blockbuster faded away.

The danger of complacency

Brands that play it safe, relying on old strategies or refusing to adapt, often find themselves left behind. In a world where customer expectations evolve rapidly, complacency is risky. Those that fail to innovate and differentiate risk losing their relevance.

Kodak's story is another example of this. Despite being a pioneer in photography, Kodak hesitated to fully embrace the digital revolution. While they clung to their traditional film business, competitors rushed into the digital space, and Kodak's failure to act decisively resulted in their decline. What was once an industry leader became an afterthought due to a lack of bold, forward-thinking differentiation.

Embracing differentiation as a survival strategy

Survival in today's market requires differentiation at the core of your brand strategy. Brands must continuously evolve, innovate, and push boundaries to maintain their uniqueness. The companies that thrive are those that aren't afraid to take risks, stand out, and offer something their competitors can't. Differentiation is not a one-time decision—it's a long-term commitment to staying relevant and irreplaceable.

Next, we'll explore how behavioral science can help brands rewire consumer perception, ensuring your brand remains distinct and memorable in the minds of your audience.

Case studies: Blockbuster and Blackberry

Blockbuster and Blackberry were once dominant brands in their respective industries. Blockbuster ruled the video rental market, and Blackberry redefined mobile communication. Yet both brands serve as cautionary tales of what happens when companies fail to differentiate and adapt. Their stories highlight the risks of clinging to outdated models and the consequences of missing opportunities to innovate.

Blockbuster: Refusal to innovate

Blockbuster, at its peak, was a household name. Its video rental stores were ubiquitous, and the brand seemed unstoppable. However, the rise of on-demand streaming and digital platforms, spearheaded by Netflix, marked the beginning of the end for Blockbuster.

Blockbuster's failure wasn't just about ignoring new technology—it was about a lack of foresight and a refusal to evolve its business model. While Netflix was gaining traction with its mail-order DVD service and later streaming platform, Blockbuster stuck to its traditional in-store rental model, charging late fees and failing to embrace the convenience and flexibility that consumers wanted.

In 2000, Blockbuster had the opportunity to purchase Netflix but turned it down, dismissing streaming as a passing trend. This shortsightedness sealed the company's fate. Blockbuster's inability to pivot, innovate, and embrace new consumer habits led to its eventual collapse. The lesson? Brands that resist change and fail to differentiate risk becoming irrelevant.

Blackberry: Disrupted by smarter innovation

Blackberry was once synonymous with mobile communication. Known for its physical keyboard and secure messaging service, Blackberry dominated the corporate and government sectors, earning a reputation for reliability. But as smartphones evolved, so did consumer expectations, and Blackberry's failure to innovate led to its downfall.

The release of the iPhone in 2007 changed the game. Touchscreens, app stores, and user-friendly interfaces appealed to a broader audience, while Blackberry continued to focus on its business-centric features, underestimating the potential of the smartphone revolution. Even as competitors like Apple and Android-based phones were reshaping the industry, Blackberry clung to its signature keyboard and operating system, failing to adapt to the touchscreen and app-driven future that consumers were embracing.

By the time Blackberry attempted to catch up with touchscreen models and modern software, it was too late. The market had shifted, and the brand's initial refusal to innovate had cost it significant market share. Once a leader in mobile technology, Blackberry is now a shadow of its former self—proof that even the most successful brands can fall if they fail to evolve with the times.

The lesson from these failures

Blockbuster and Blackberry both serve as stark reminders that no brand, no matter how dominant, is immune to extinction if it refuses to innovate. In both cases, the failure to differentiate their offerings in response to shifting consumer behavior and technological advancements led to their decline. The lesson for today's brands is clear: staying relevant requires continuous adaptation, foresight, and the willingness to embrace bold changes.

Next, we'll explore how behavioral science plays a role in branding, helping companies influence consumer perception and create lasting impressions.

CHAPTER 10

SUSTAINING DIFFERENTIATION

Staying relevant while staying true

Differentiating your brand is challenging, but maintaining that differentiation over time can be even harder. As markets evolve and competitors catch up, what once made you unique can quickly become commonplace. The challenge is figuring out how to sustain differentiation without losing sight of your core identity. Brands that navigate this balance successfully don't just survive—they thrive in the long run.

Evolving without losing your essence

Staying relevant requires constant adaptation, but it's essential to do so without straying too far from what made your brand unique in the first place. The key is understanding which elements of your differentiation should remain fixed and which can evolve to meet new market demands.

Take LEGO, for example. The company built its success on creativity, imagination, and play. Over the years, LEGO has evolved by embracing new themes, licensing partnerships (like Star Wars and Marvel), and digital experiences like LEGO video games and apps. However, the brand has remained true to its core purpose—building creativity through play. LEGO's ability to innovate while maintaining its essence is why it has sustained differentiation and remained relevant to new generations of consumers.

Consistent innovation

Differentiation is not a one-time achievement. Brands that want to sustain their unique position must continue to innovate, even after they've established themselves as market leaders. Innovation doesn't always have to mean groundbreaking technology; it can also mean improving customer experience, finding new ways to engage your audience, or refining your product offering in response to changing needs.

Nike is an example of a brand that consistently sustains differentiation through innovation. Whether by developing performance-enhancing technologies like Nike Air or expanding into sustainability initiatives with Nike Grind, the company continuously evolves its offerings. Yet, Nike remains consistent in its focus on empowering athletes of all levels, which ensures they stay true to their brand's core identity.

Staying customer-focused

One of the best ways to sustain differentiation is by maintaining a close relationship with your audience. Consumer preferences and expectations evolve over time, and brands that listen to their customers are better positioned to adapt without losing their uniqueness. This level of responsiveness keeps a brand from becoming stagnant and ensures that its relevance is tied to the ongoing needs of its audience.

Sustaining differentiation also means knowing when to pivot. When it becomes clear that the market is shifting, brands that are agile and willing to change while keeping their core values intact have the best chance of staying ahead of the curve.

Next, we'll dive into how brands can navigate the tricky decision of whether to pivot or double down when facing market shifts and competition.

Pivot or double down

At some point, every brand faces a critical decision: should you stick with what's worked so far, or pivot to adapt to changing market conditions? Knowing when to double down on your core strengths and when to shift directions can be the difference between sustaining success and falling behind. The challenge is recognizing which path will keep your brand differentiated in an evolving landscape.

When doubling down makes sense

Staying the course can be the right choice when your brand's core identity remains relevant and continues to resonate with your audience. Sometimes, what looks like external pressure to change is just noise, and doubling down on your unique strengths can help your brand maintain its position in the market. However, this requires a clear understanding of what makes your brand valuable and a commitment to refining and strengthening that core offering.

Take Patagonia, for instance. As a brand committed to environmental sustainability, Patagonia has remained true to its mission even as the outdoor apparel industry has grown more competitive. Instead of pivoting toward fast fashion or mass production to compete on volume, Patagonia doubled down on sustainability, making product longevity, ethical sourcing, and environmental activism central to their brand. This consistency not only reinforced their differentiation but also deepened customer loyalty among those who shared their values.

When a pivot is necessary

Sometimes, the market shifts, consumer preferences evolve, or competitors catch up—and sticking to your original strategy becomes risky. In these situations, a pivot can breathe new life into your brand, allowing you to maintain differentiation while staying relevant. A successful pivot doesn't mean abandoning your brand's essence, but rather adjusting the way you deliver your value in a way that aligns with new trends or technologies.

Take Microsoft, a company once known primarily for its Windows operating system and Office software. As the tech landscape shifted toward cloud computing, Microsoft pivoted to focus on cloud-based services like Azure. By expanding into cloud computing while staying true to its mission of empowering individuals and businesses through technology, Microsoft positioned itself as a leader in the tech industry once again. This pivot ensured they remained relevant in an evolving market without losing their core identity.

The risks of indecision

The greatest danger for any brand is indecision. Brands that hesitate, unsure whether to pivot or stay the course, often end up doing neither effectively. They risk becoming irrelevant by sticking too closely to outdated strategies or by making half-hearted changes that don't fully address market shifts.

Kodak's failure to pivot quickly enough when digital photography overtook film is a well-known example. Even though Kodak invented the first digital camera, they delayed fully embracing digital technology for fear of cannibalizing their film business. By the time they made a move, it was too late, and they had lost their position as the leader in photography.

Making the right decision

The decision to pivot or double down comes down to understanding your brand's core strengths and staying attuned to the needs and expectations of your audience. Brands that successfully navigate this decision are those that stay flexible, listen to the market, and remain focused on their long-term vision. Whether doubling down on what sets you apart or adjusting to meet new demands, the goal is the same: sustaining differentiation in a way that keeps your brand relevant and valuable.

Next, we'll explore how brands can keep their differentiation fresh over time, ensuring that what makes them unique doesn't grow stale in a changing market.

Keeping your brand fresh

Differentiation may set your brand apart, but staying fresh is what ensures your brand continues to captivate and engage your audience over time. Markets change, trends evolve, and consumer expectations shift. Brands that succeed over the long term don't just rely on their initial uniqueness—they consistently refresh their image, offerings, and messaging to remain relevant while staying true to their core identity.

Innovating within your core identity

One of the most effective ways to keep your brand fresh is by evolving from within. Rather than straying too far from what makes your brand unique, innovation can breathe new life into your existing strengths. This kind of internal evolution ensures that your brand stays relevant without losing its essence.

Take LEGO as an example. The brand has remained a creative powerhouse for decades, yet it continuously reinvents itself with new product lines, digital experiences, and partnerships with major franchises like Harry Potter and Star Wars. By integrating these new elements while staying true to its core mission—building creativity through play—LEGO keeps its brand fresh, attracting new generations of fans while maintaining loyalty among long-time customers.

Evolving customer engagement

Another way to keep your brand fresh is through ongoing, thoughtful engagement with your audience. As customer behaviors change, so should the ways you interact with them. This doesn't mean changing your values, but it does mean updating the way you communicate, deliver content, and create experiences that resonate with current preferences.

Take Nike's approach to engaging its community. While the brand's core identity remains rooted in athleticism and empowerment, it continuously evolves its digital platforms to offer personalized training experiences, virtual challenges, and community engagement through apps like Nike Training Club. By keeping customer interaction dynamic and modern, Nike ensures its brand feels current, even as its foundational message stays consistent.

Avoiding the trap of stagnation

The biggest risk to long-term differentiation is stagnation. Brands that rest on their laurels, relying on their initial success without ongoing evolution, eventually lose relevance. Staying fresh requires an ongoing effort to assess where your brand stands in the market and whether your differentiation still resonates with consumers.

Consider Gap, a brand that once dominated the casual apparel space. Over time, Gap failed to evolve its image and offerings in response to changing fashion trends and consumer behaviors. As a result, the brand became stale, losing relevance and market share to more fashion-forward competitors. The lesson? No matter how strong your brand is initially, failing to adapt can lead to a slow decline.

Refreshing your brand without alienating your audience

It's important to remember that staying fresh doesn't mean changing everything. If your brand evolves too dramatically, you risk alienating loyal customers who are attached to your existing identity. The key is to refresh in ways that feel natural and aligned with your brand's core values, ensuring that innovation feels like an extension of your mission, not a departure from it.

Maintaining a balance between consistency and evolution is what allows brands to stay fresh while preserving their identity. Successful brands are those that continually find new ways to innovate and engage, all while staying true to what made them unique in the first place.

CONCLUSION

DIFFERENTIATION IS FOREVER

The infinite pursuit of staying remarkable

Differentiation is not a one-time achievement—it's a constant journey. Brands that succeed in standing out know that the real challenge begins after they've carved out their unique space in the market. The pursuit of staying remarkable requires ongoing commitment, creativity, and the courage to evolve while staying true to your core. The moment you become complacent, you risk blending into the sea of competitors, losing the edge that once set you apart.

Consistent innovation as a mindset

Staying remarkable means embracing innovation, not as an occasional effort, but as a mindset that permeates every aspect of your brand. The world is constantly shifting, with new technologies, consumer behaviors, and cultural trends emerging all the time. Brands that commit to differentiation don't just respond to these changes—they anticipate them.

Think of innovation as an ongoing process of improvement, where you're always looking for ways to refine your product, enhance customer experiences, and deepen your connection with your audience. It's about more than just introducing new features or products—it's about rethinking how your brand can consistently provide value in a way that only you can.

Adapting while remaining authentic

While innovation is essential, it's equally important to remain true to your brand's core values. Staying remarkable isn't about chasing every trend or trying to appeal to everyone—it's about evolving in ways that are authentic to your identity. Brands that successfully adapt without losing their essence are the ones that sustain long-term differentiation.

The key is to strike a balance between evolution and consistency. You must remain flexible enough to grow and adapt, while still maintaining the integrity of what made your brand special in the first place. Customers are drawn to brands that feel both fresh and familiar—brands that surprise them with new ideas but stay grounded in their core mission.

The pursuit never ends

Being remarkable isn't something you achieve and then check off your list—it's a continuous pursuit. Brands that truly stand the test of time are those that understand the journey never ends. They remain curious, driven by the desire to keep exploring new ways to create, connect, and inspire.

The pursuit of staying remarkable also means being unafraid to take risks, knowing that not every attempt will succeed, but understanding that stagnation is the real danger. Bold brands are the ones that dare to push boundaries, even when the outcome is uncertain.

Ultimately, staying remarkable requires a commitment to always striving for more. It's about pushing the limits of what your brand can be and never settling for the ordinary.

Next, we'll look at the key takeaways for lasting differentiation, distilling the essential lessons from this journey into practical strategies you can apply to ensure your brand remains remarkable, no matter what changes come.

Key takeaways for lasting differentiation

Differentiation is the foundation of brand success, but keeping it alive requires constant vigilance and thoughtful strategy. Throughout this journey, we've explored the many ways brands can stand out and the challenges they face in maintaining that unique position. To ensure your brand remains not just different, but remarkable, here are the key lessons you should carry forward:

1. Know what makes you different—and own it

The first step to lasting differentiation is a deep understanding of what truly sets your brand apart. It's not just about surface-level differences, like product features or pricing. It's about identifying your brand's core identity and ensuring that it permeates everything you do. Whether it's a unique value proposition, an innovative approach to customer experience, or a mission that resonates deeply with your audience, knowing what makes you different gives you the foundation to build on.

Brands that fail to differentiate at a fundamental level risk becoming commodities, indistinguishable from the competition. Own your identity, stay true to it, and make sure your audience knows why you're different from everyone else.

2. Adapt without losing your essence

The market will change, and so will your customers' expectations. The brands that endure are those that stay flexible, willing to evolve with the times without losing the core of what made them special in the first place. Balancing innovation with authenticity is critical. Adapt your products, services, and messaging to reflect new realities, but always stay grounded in your brand's mission.

Remember, adaptation doesn't mean reinventing your brand from scratch. It means growing in ways that align with your values and finding new opportunities to bring those values to life in fresh, compelling ways.

3. Innovate continuously

Differentiation isn't static. What makes your brand unique today might not be enough tomorrow. The brands that sustain their unique position are those that embrace continuous innovation—not just in their products, but in how they engage with customers, create experiences, and respond to the market. Successful brands never stop looking for ways to improve, surprise, and delight their audience.

Whether it's exploring new technologies, redefining customer experiences, or introducing groundbreaking ideas, constant innovation is what keeps your brand from becoming stagnant. Bold moves keep your audience interested, and calculated risks can open up new opportunities for growth.

4. Build emotional connections

Differentiation isn't just about standing out visually or functionally—it's about creating emotional connections that make customers feel something meaningful about your brand. People don't just buy products; they buy into stories, experiences, and values that resonate with their personal beliefs. When your brand forms a genuine connection with its audience, it transcends the competition.

Storytelling, purpose-driven missions, and authentic engagement are key tools in building those emotional ties. Brands that tap into what their customers care about and stand for something beyond profit are the ones that create lasting loyalty.

5. Commit to the journey

Finally, the most important takeaway is that differentiation is an ongoing process, not a one-time achievement. Brands that remain remarkable are those that commit to the long haul, consistently refining, adapting, and pushing boundaries. The moment you stop investing in what makes you different is the moment you start to fade into the background.

It's a relentless pursuit, but one that leads to long-term success. Brands that embrace the challenge of continuous differentiation are the ones that not only survive but thrive in even the most competitive markets.

As we wrap up this exploration of differentiation, let's look to the future and examine how the changing world will continue to shape the way brands stand out.

The future of standing out in a changing world

The business landscape is constantly evolving, and so are the ways in which brands differentiate themselves. What worked a decade ago may no longer apply, and the strategies of today will inevitably change tomorrow. As technology advances, consumer expectations shift, and global events reshape industries, the future of differentiation will require agility, innovation, and a deep understanding of what truly resonates with customers.

The rise of purpose-driven brands

More than ever, consumers are looking for brands that align with their values. The next generation of customers—particularly Millennials and Gen Z—demand more from companies than just products and services. They want to support brands that stand for something, whether that's social justice, sustainability, or ethical business practices. Purpose-driven brands that can clearly communicate their mission will find it easier to create lasting emotional connections with their audience.

In the future, differentiation will increasingly be about your brand's impact on the world. Whether it's through environmental initiatives, community engagement, or transparency in business practices, standing out will require more than just offering a good product—it will mean standing for something meaningful.

Technology as a differentiator

Technology will continue to play a pivotal role in how brands differentiate. From artificial intelligence to augmented reality, the tools at a brand's disposal are expanding, and so are the possibilities for creating unique experiences. Personalization, once a novel feature, will become the baseline expectation, and brands that use technology creatively will have the edge.

We're already seeing how brands leverage technology to provide immersive experiences that go beyond traditional marketing. In the future, virtual spaces, enhanced personalization, and AI-driven engagement will allow brands to connect with customers in new and innovative ways. The brands that adopt these technologies early, and in ways that align with their core values, will set themselves apart.

The demand for authenticity

As digital interactions grow, so does the demand for authenticity. In a world where technology can sometimes feel impersonal, brands that maintain a human touch will stand out. Customers are increasingly skeptical of overly polished, manufactured messages and are drawn to transparency and real, meaningful interactions.

In the future, successful brands will be those that balance the convenience and innovation of digital tools with the warmth and authenticity of personal connection. Maintaining trust will be crucial, and brands that can communicate openly, act transparently, and engage with customers on a human level will create deeper loyalty.

Global shifts and adaptability

The global landscape is changing rapidly—political, social, and environmental factors are increasingly shaping consumer behavior. Brands that can remain agile and adapt to these shifts will be the ones that continue to thrive. Whether responding to a global pandemic, adjusting to new regulations, or aligning with changing social norms, adaptability will be key to long-term differentiation.

The future will reward brands that stay flexible and open to change, without losing sight of their core values. The ability to pivot when needed, while maintaining a strong sense of purpose, will separate the leaders from the followers.

Continuous evolution

Looking ahead, the brands that succeed will be the ones that embrace continuous evolution. Differentiation is not a destination—it's an ongoing process of adapting, innovating, and reimagining what your brand can offer. As the world changes, so must your approach to standing out. The brands that commit to this never-ending pursuit of relevance and uniqueness will be the ones that lead the way.

In a world where the only constant is change, standing out will require more than just one great idea. It will require the courage to evolve, the vision to anticipate what's next, and the drive to keep pushing boundaries—while always staying true to what makes your brand remarkable.

REFERENCES

Aaker, D. A. (2021). Building strong brands. Free Press.

Anwar, A., Gulzar, A., & Sohail, F. B. (2022). Impact of celebrity endorsements on consumer brand perception and loyalty in the fashion industry. Journal of Fashion Marketing and Management, 26(2), 350-370. https://doi.org/10.1108/JFMM-05-2021-0115

Berthon, P., Pitt, L., & Campbell, C. (2019). Brand management in the digital economy: Foundations and future directions. Journal of Brand Management, 26(4), 317-331. https://doi.org/10.1057/s41262-019-00158-x

Chae, S., & Ko, E. (2021). Brand management in the era of social media: Big data and artificial intelligence for enhancing brand equity. Journal of Business Research, 129, 357-366. https://doi.org/10.1016/j.jbusres.2021.03.030

Chung, J., & Kim, S. (2023). Brand heritage and consumer loyalty: The moderating effect of brand innovativeness. Journal of Business Research, 147, 313-324. https://doi.org/10.1016/j.jbusres.2022.12.017

Dwivedi, Y. K., Ismagilova, E., & Hughes, D. L. (2021). Setting the future of digital and social media marketing research: Perspectives and research propositions. International Journal of Information Management, 59, 102168. https://doi.org/10.1016/j.ijinfomgt.2021.102168

Erdem, T., Swait, J., & Valenzuela, A. (2020). Brand credibility, perceived quality, and choice. Journal of Consumer Research, 47(1), 3-22. https://doi.org/10.1093/jcr/ucaa008

Fuchs, C., & Schreier, M. (2021). Customer empowerment and brand co-creation: A theoretical framework. Journal of Marketing Research, 58(3), 455-470. https://doi.org/10.1177/0022243720980514

Fournier, S., Breazeale, M., & Avery, J. (2019). Strong brands, strong relationships. Routledge.

Gupta, S., & Zeithaml, V. A. (2020). Brand value co-creation in digital and social media environments. Journal of Interactive Marketing, 50, 1-15. https://doi.org/10.1016/j.intmar.2020.02.002

Holt, D. B. (2016). Branding in the age of social media. Harvard Business Review, 94(3), 40-50.

Kapferer, J. N. (2012). The new strategic brand management: Advanced insights and strategic thinking (5th ed.). Kogan Page.

Keller, K. L. (2019). Managing the growth trade-off: Challenges and opportunities in luxury branding. Journal of Brand Management, 26(4), 383-394. https://doi.org/10.1057/s41262-018-0125-0

Kotler, P., Keller, K. L., & Chernev, A. (2020). Marketing management (16th ed.). Pearson.

Palmatier, R. W., Houston, M. B., & Hulland, J. (2019). Review articles: Purpose, process, and structure. Journal of the Academy of Marketing Science, 47(1), 1-5. https://doi.org/10.1007/s11747-018-0598-0

Ries, A., & Trout, J. (2001). Positioning: The battle for your mind. McGraw-Hill.

Romaniuk, J., & Sharp, B. (2022). Building distinctive brand assets: The case of Coca-Cola and Pepsi. Marketing Science, 41(1), 123-137. https://doi.org/10.1287/mksc.2021.1297

Sasmita, J., & Suki, N. M. (2020). Young consumers' insights on brand equity: Effects of brand association, brand loyalty, and brand awareness. Journal of Global Marketing, 33(5), 307-319. https://doi.org/10.1080/08911762.2020.1718305

Shapiro, S., & Nielsen, J. (2020). Brand recall and recognition in the digital age: Cognitive mechanisms. Journal of Consumer Psychology, 30(3), 463-478. https://doi.org/10.1002/jcpy.1182

Sinek, S. (2009). Start with why: How great leaders inspire everyone to take action. Portfolio.

Teece, D. J. (2020). Dynamic capabilities and strategic management: Organizing for innovation and growth. Strategic Management Journal, 41(1), 22-40. https://doi.org/10.1002/smj.3093

Teixeira, T. S., Wedel, M., & Pieters, R. (2020). Moment-to-moment optimal branding in TV commercials: Preventing avoidance by pulsing. Journal of Marketing Research, 57(6), 1092-1109. https://doi.org/10.1177/0022243720928133

Törmälä, M., & Geyskens, I. (2020). The irony of honesty: How firm honesty in pricing increases sales. Journal of Marketing, 84(2), 36-51. https://doi.org/10.1177/0022242919899351

Zhu, R. J., Chen, X., & Su, S. (2022). Brand warmth and competence in service brands: The role of corporate social responsibility. Journal of Service Research, 25(1), 32-48. https://doi.org/10.1177/10946705211007089

Dwivedi, Y. K., Rana, N. P., Jeyaraj, A., Clement, M., & Williams, M. D. (2020). Re-examining the unified theory of acceptance and use of technology (UTAUT): Towards a revised theoretical model. Information Systems Frontiers, 22(1), 49-75. https://doi.org/10.1007/s10796-019-09990-2

ABOUT THE AUTHOR
MARCOS G. FIGUEIRA

Marcos Figueira is a seasoned marketing and branding expert with over 30 years of experience across diverse industries and global markets. As a partner at Wyse since the 1990s, he has helped businesses build impactful brands that resonate with their audiences. Alongside his consulting work, Marcos has been an MBA professor at leading business schools since 2012, sharing his deep knowledge of marketing strategy. With an MBA, MSc., and PhD, Marcos blends practical expertise with academic rigor, offering unique insights into branding, marketing, and business growth. Today, he continues to thrive as a consultant, speaker, professor, and published author.

THANK YOU!

Other Books from the Author

The Cognitive Marketing: How to Influence Consumer Perception and Behavior

Growth Marketing: The Playbook for Startups and Beyond

The 6E's of Branding: A Framework for Brand Strategists

Marcos G. Figueira
Instagram
@marcosfigueira
LinkedIn
@marcosfigueira

https://marcosfigueira.com
https://wyse.com.br